Ecosocialism

Ecosocialism
A Radical Alternative
to Capitalist Catastrophe

Michael Löwy

Haymarket Books
Chicago, Illinois

Published in 2015 by
Haymarket Books
P.O. Box 180165
Chicago, IL 60618
773-583-7884
www.haymarketbooks.org
info@haymarketbooks.org

ISBN: 978-1-60846-471-5

Trade distribution:
In the US, Consortium Book Sales and Distribution, www.cbsd.com
In Canada, Publishers Group Canada, www.pgcbooks.ca
In the UK, Turnaround Publisher Services, www.turnaround-psl.com
All other countries, Publishers Group Worldwide, www.pgw.com

This book was published with the generous support of Lannan Foundation
and Wallace Action Fund.

Cover design by Christine Knowlton.

Library of Congress Cataloging-in-Publication data is available.

Contents

Preface   vii
Before the Flood: The Political Challenge of Ecosocialism

Chapter One: 1
What Is Ecosocialism?

Chapter Two: 19
Ecosocialism and Democratic Planning

Chapter Three: 41
Ecology and Advertising

Chapter Four: 53
Chico Mendes and the Brazilian Struggle
for the Amazonian Forest

Chapter Five: 61
Ecosocial Struggles of Indigenous Peoples

Appendix 1:   77
International Ecosocialist Manifesto (2001)

Appendix 2:   83
The Belém Declaration (2009)

Appendix 3:   99
Copenhagen 2049 (2009)

Appendix 4:   101
The Lima Ecosocialist Declaration (2014)

Notes   105

Index   111

Before the Flood: The Political Challenge of Ecosocialism

Ecosocialism is a political current based on an essential insight: that preserving the ecological equilibrium of the planet and therefore an environment favorable to living species, including ours, is incompatible with the expansive and destructive logic of the capitalist system. The pursuit of "growth" under the aegis of capital will lead us in short range—the next decades—to a catastrophe without precedent in human history: global warming.

James Hansen is NASA's chief climatologist and one of the world's greatest specialists on climate change; the George W. Bush administration tried, in vain, to prevent him from publishing his investigations. Hansen wrote this in the first paragraph of his book *Storms of My Grandchildren: The Truth about the Coming Climate Catastrophe and Our Last Chance to Save Humanity* (2009):

Planet Earth, creation, the world in which civilization developed, the world with climate patterns that we know and stable shore- lines, is in imminent peril. The urgency of the situation crystal- lized only in the past few years. We have now clear evidence of the crisis. . . . The startling conclusion is that continued exploita- tion of all fossil fuels on Earth threatens not only the other mil- lions of species on the planet but also the survival of humanity itself—and the timetable is shorter than we thought.

This understanding is largely shared across lands and conti- nents. In a well-informed essay, "How the Rich Destroy the Planet," the French ecologist Hervé Kempf gives us a true picture of the dis- aster being prepared: beyond a certain threshold, which may arrive much sooner than predicted, the climate system may run away ir- reversibly; we cannot rule out a sudden and brutal change, with temperatures rising by several degrees and attaining unbearable lev- els. Faced with this knowledge, confirmed by scientists and shared by millions of citizens around the world, what are the powerful doing, the oligarchy of billionaires that rules the world economy? The social system that presently dominates human societies, capi- talism, blindly and stubbornly resists changes that are indispensable if we are to preserve the dignity of human existence. A predatory and greedy ruling class refuses any attempt at an effective transfor- mation; almost all spheres of power and influence submit to a pseudorealism that pretends that any alternative is impossible and that the only way forward is "growth." This oligarchy, obsessed by conspicuous consumption—as Thorstein Veblen described many years ago—is indifferent to the degradation of living conditions for the majority of human beings and blind to the seriousness of the biosphere's poisoning.

The planet's "decision makers"—billionaires, managers, bankers, investors, ministers, business executives, and "experts"—shaped by the shortsighted and narrow-minded rationality of the system and obsessed by the imperatives of growth and expansion, the struggle for market positions, competitiveness, and profit margins, seem to follow the precept King Louis XV proclaimed a few years before the French Revolution: "After me, the Flood." The twenty-first-century Flood, like the biblical one, may take the form of an inexorable rise of the waters, drowning the coastal towns of human civilization under the waves: New York, London, Venice, Amsterdam, Rio de Janeiro, Hong Kong. . . .

The spectacular failure of all international conferences on climate change—Copenhagen, Cancún, Doha, Rio—illustrates this voluntary blindness: the greatest polluters, beginning with the United States, China, Canada, and Australia, have refused any commitment to a concrete reduction, even a minimal one, of carbon dioxide emissions. The weak measures more "enlightened" capitalist governments have taken so far—such as the Kyoto agreements and the European climate-action package, with their "flexibility mechanisms" and emission-trading schemes—are quite unable to confront the dramatic challenge of climate change. The same applies to the "technological" solutions privileged by President Obama and the European Union: "electric cars," "agro-fuels," "clean carbon," and so on. As Marx predicted in *The German Ideology*, productive forces in capitalism are becoming destructive forces, creating the risk of physical annihilation for millions of human beings—a scenario even worse than the "tropical holocausts" of the nineteenth century studied by Mike Davis.

One word about another marvelous, "clean and secure" technology, favored not only by the powers that be but also, unfortunately, by some ecologists (Monbiot, Hansen, Lovelock), as an alternative to fossil resources: nuclear energy. After the terrifying Chernobyl accident in 1986, the Western atomic lobby found its answer: this was the result of bureaucratic, incompetent, and inefficient management of nuclear plants in the Soviet Union. "Such a thing couldn't happen among us." After the 2011 accident in Fukushima, Japan, this kind of argument lost all currency: TEPCO, which owns the Japanese nuclear plant, is one of the largest private capitalist enterprises in the country. The fact is that insecurity is inherent to nuclear energy: accidents are statistically inevitable. Sooner or later, new Chernobyls and new Fukushimas will take place, provoked by human error, internal dysfunction, earthquakes, tsunamis, airplane accidents, or other unpredictable events. Moreover, replacing fossil-fueled plants with nuclear ones on a world scale would mean building hundreds of new such plants, inevitably increasing the probability of more accidents.

◆ ◆ ◆

What is the alternative solution? Individual asceticism and penitence, as so many ecologists seem to propose? Drastically reducing consumption? The cultural criticism of consumerism is necessary but insufficient: one has to challenge the mode of production itself. Only a collective and democratic reorganization of the productive system could, at the same time, satisfy real social needs, reduce labor time, suppress useless and/or dangerous production, and replace fossil fuels with renewable energy sources. All this requires deep incursions into capitalist propriety, a radical extension of the public sector, and, in a word, a democratic, ecosocialist plan.

The central premise of ecosocialism, already suggested by the term itself, is that nonecological socialism is a dead end and a nonsocialist ecology cannot confront the present ecological crisis. The ecosocialist proposition of combining the "red" (the Marxist critique of capital and the project of an alternative society) and the "green" (the ecological critique of productivism) has nothing to do with the so-called "red-green" governmental coalitions between social democrats and certain green parties, on the basis of a social-liberal program of capitalist management. Ecosocialism is a radical proposition— i.e., one that deals with the roots of the ecological crisis—which distinguishes itself from the productivist varieties of socialism in the twentieth century (either social democracy or the Stalinist brand of "communism") as well as from the ecological currents that accommodate themselves in one way or another to the capitalist system. This radical proposition aims not only to transform the relations of production, the productive apparatus, and the dominant consumption patterns but to create a new way of life, breaking with the foundations of the modern Western capitalist/industrial civilization.

I cannot develop the history of ecosocialism in this preface. I will, however, mention a few stepping-stones. They concern mainly the eco-Marxist tendency, but one can find—for example, in Murray Bookchin's *Anarchist Social Ecology*, in Arne Naess's leftist version of deep ecology, and among certain "degrowth" authors such as Paul Ariès—radically anticapitalist analysis and alternative solutions that are not too far from ecosocialism.

The idea of an ecological socialism—or a socialist ecology— didn't start really to develop until the 1970s, when it appeared, under different forms, in the writings of certain pioneers of a "Red-Green" way of thinking: Manuel Sacristán in Spain, Raymond Williams in the United Kingdom, André Gorz and Jean-Paul Deléage in France, Barry Commoner in the United States (preceded by Rachel Carson in the 1960s), and Wolfgang Harich in East Germany, to name a few. The word *ecosocialism* came into use mainly after the 1980s, when it appeared in the German Green Party, a leftist tendency that designated itself as ecosocialist; its main spokespersons were Rainer Trampert and Thomas Ebermann. At the same time came the book *The Alternative*, by an East German dissident, Rudolf Bahro: a radical critique of the Soviet and East German model in the name of an ecological socialism. During the 1980s the US economist James O'Connor developed in his writings a new Marxist ecological approach and founded the journal *Capitalism Nature Socialism*. Also during this period Frieder Otto Wolf, member of the European Parliament and one of the main leaders of the left wing of the German Green Party, would contribute—together with Pierre Juquin, a former French Communist leader converted to the red-green perspective—to a book called *Europe's Green Alternative* (1992), a sort of first ecosocialist European program.

Meanwhile, in Spain, followers of Manuel Sacristán, such as Francisco Fernández Buey, developed socialist ecological arguments in the Barcelona journal *Mientras Tanto* (*In the Meantime*). In 2001 the Fourth International, a Marxist/revolutionary current present in several countries that was founded by Leon Trotsky in 1938, adopted an ecosocialist resolution titled "Ecology and Socialist Revolution" at its world congress. In the same year, Joel Kovel and the author of this book published an international "Ecosocialist Manifesto" that was widely discussed and inspired, in 2007, the founding in Paris of the International Ecosocialist Network (IEN). A second ecosocialist manifesto discussing global warming, the Belém Declaration, was signed by hundreds of people from dozens of countries and distributed at the World Social Forum in Belém in the state of Pará, Brazil, in 2009. A few months later, during the UN International Conference on Climate Change in Copenhagen, the IEN disseminated an illustrated comic strip, *Copenhagen 2049*, among a hundred thousand demonstrators gathered under the banner "Change the System, Not the Climate!"

To this must be added, in the United States, the work of John Bellamy Foster, Fred Magdoff, Paul Burkett, and their friends from the well-known North American left journal *Monthly Review*, who argue for a Marxist ecology; the continued activity of *Capitalism Nature Socialism* under the editorship of Joel Kovel, author of *The Enemy of Nature* (2002); and, more recently, of Salvatore Engel-Di Mauro and of the young circle of activists called Ecosocialist Horizons and its cofounder Quincy Saul, who recently edited an ecosocialist comic book called *Truth and Dare* (2014). There have been many important books, among which one of the most inclusive is Chris Williams's *Ecology and Socialism* (2010). Equally important, in other countries, have been the ecosocialist and ecofeminist writings of Ariel Salleh and Terisa Turner; the journal *Canadian Dimension*, edited by ecosocialists Ian Angus and Cy Gonick; the writings of the Belgian Marxist Daniel Tanuro on climate change and the dead end of "green capitalism"; the research of French authors linked to the global justice movement, such as Jean-Marie Harribey; the philosophical writings of Arno Münster, an ecosocialist follower of Ernst Bloch and André Gorz; and the recent *Manifeste Ecosocialiste* (2014), edited by a committee of activists belonging to the radical wing of the French Front de Gauche (Left Front) and the 2014 European Ecosocialist Conference, which took place in Geneva.

It would be a mistake to conclude that ecosocialism is limited to Europe and North America: there is lively ecosocialist activity and discussion in Latin America. In Brazil, a local ecosocialist network has been established, with scholars and activists from various parties, unions, and peasant movements; in Mexico, there have been several publications discussing ecosocialism. The well-known Peruvian revolutionary leader Hugo Blanco has been active in the IEN, emphasizing the common agenda of the Indigenous movements and ecosocialism. In 2014 there were ecosocialist conferences in Quito and Caracas. Last but not least, there is growing interest in ecosocialism in China; Bellamy Foster's and Kovel's books have been translated into Chinese, and Chinese universities have organized several conferences on ecosocialism in the last few years.

It is important to emphasize that ecosocialism is a project for the future, a horizon of the possible, a radical anticapitalist alternative, but also—and inseparably—an agenda of action hic et nunc, here and now, around concrete and immediate proposals. Any victories, however partial or limited, that slow down climate change and ecological degradation are stepping-stones for more victories: they develop our confidence and organization to push for more. There is no guarantee that the ecosocialist alternative will triumph; very little can be expected from the powers that be. The only hope lies in mobilizations from below, like in Seattle in 1999, which saw the coming together of "turtles and teamsters" (ecologists and trade unionists) and the birth of the global justice movement, or Copenhagen in 2009, or Cochabamba, Bolivia, in 2010, when thirty thousand delegates from Indigenous, peasant, labor, and ecologist movements in Latin America and around the world participated in the World People's Conference on Climate Change and the Rights of Mother Earth.

The present collection of articles is not a systematic presentation of the ecosocialist ideas and practices, but a more modest attempt to explore some of its theoretical aspects and proposals as well as some concrete experiences of struggle. The book represents, of course, the opinions of its author, which don't necessarily coincide with those of other ecosocialist thinkers or networks. There is no intention here to codify a doctrine or any sort of orthodoxy. One of the virtues of ecosocialism is precisely its diversity—its plurality, the multiplicity of its perspectives and approaches, which are often convergent or complementary but also sometimes divergent and even contradictory.

CHAPTER ONE

What Is Ecosocialism?

Translated by Eric Canepa

The reigning capitalist system is bringing the planet's inhabitants a long list of irreparable calamities. Witness: exponential growth of air pollution in big cities and across rural landscapes; fouled drinking water; global warming, with the incipient melting of the polar ice caps and the increase of "natural" extreme weather–related catastrophes; the deterioration of the ozone layer; the increasing destruction of tropical rainforests; the rapid decrease of biodiversity through the extinction of thousands of species; the exhausting of the soil; desertification; the unmanageable accumulation of waste, especially nuclear; the multiplication of nuclear accidents along with the threat of a new—and perhaps more destructive—Chernobyl; food contamination, genetic engineering, "mad cow," and hormone-injected beef. All the warning signs are red: it is clear that the insatiable quest for profits,

Originally published in *Capitalism Nature Socialism* 16(2), June 2005.

the productivist and mercantile logic of capitalist/industrial civilization is leading us into an ecological disaster of incalculable proportions. This is not to give in to "catastrophism" but to verify that the dynamic of infinite "growth" brought about by capitalist expansion is threatening the natural foundations of human life on the planet.

How should we react to this danger? Socialism and ecology—or at least some of its currents—share objective goals that imply a questioning of this economic automatism, of the reign of quantification, of production as a goal in itself, of the dictatorship of money, of the reduction of the social universe to the calculations of profitability and the needs of capital accumulation. Both socialism and ecology appeal to qualitative values—for the socialists, use value, the satisfaction of needs, social equality; for the ecologists, protecting nature and ecological balance. Both conceive of the economy as "embedded" in the environment—a social environment or a natural environment.

That said, basic differences have until now separated the "reds" from the "greens," the Marxists from the ecologists. Ecologists accuse Marx and Engels of productivism. Is this justified? Yes and no.

No, to the extent that no one has denounced the capitalist logic of production for production's sake—as well as the accumulation of capital, wealth, and commodities as goals in themselves—as vehemently as Marx did. The very idea of socialism—contrary to its miserable bureaucratic deformations—is that of production of use values, of goods necessary to the satisfaction of human needs. For Marx, the supreme goal of technical progress is not the infinite accumulation of goods ("having") but the reduction of the working day and the accumulation of free time ("being").

Yes, to the extent that one often sees in Marx and Engels (and all the more in later Marxism) a tendency to make the "development of the productive forces" the principal vector of progress, along with an insufficiently critical attitude toward industrial civilization, notably in its destructive relationship to the environment.

In reality, one can find material in the writings of Marx and Engels to support both interpretations. The ecological issue is, in my opinion, the great challenge for a renewal of Marxist thought at the threshold of the twenty-first century. It requires that Marxists undertake a deep critical revision of their traditional conception of "productive forces" and that they break radically with the ideology of linear progress and with the technological and economic paradigm of modern industrial civilization.

◆ ◆ ◆

Walter Benjamin was one of the first Marxists in the twentieth century to articulate this question. In 1928, in his book *One-Way Street*, he denounced as an "imperialist doctrine" the idea of the domination of nature and proposed a new conception of technology as a "mastery of the relations between nature and humanity." Some years later, in *On the Concept of History*, he proposed enriching historical materialism with the ideas of Fourier, that utopian visionary who dreamt of "labor, which, far from exploiting nature, would be capable of awakening the creations that slept in its womb."

Today Marxism is still far from having made up for its backwardness in this regard. Nevertheless, certain lines of thinking are beginning to tackle the problem. A fertile trail has been opened up by the American ecologist and "Marxist-Polanyist" James O'Connor. He proposes that we add to Marx's first contradiction of capitalism (that between the forces and relations of production) a second contradiction (that between productive forces and conditions of production) which takes into account workers, urban space, and nature. Through its expansionist dynamic, O'Connor points out, capital endangers or destroys its own conditions, beginning with the natural environment—a possibility that Marx did not adequately consider.

Another interesting approach is one suggested in a recent piece by the Italian "eco-Marxist" Tiziano Bagarollo:

> The formula according to which there is a transformation of potentially productive forces into effectively destructive ones, above all in regard to the environment, seems more appropriate and meaningful than the well-known scheme of the contradiction between (dynamic) forces of production and relations of production (that are fetters on the former). Moreover, this formula provides a critical, non-apologetic, foundation for economic, technological, and scientific development and therefore the elaboration of a "differentiated" (Ernst Bloch) concept of progress.

Whether Marxist or not, the traditional labor movement in Europe—unions, social-democratic and communist parties—remains profoundly shaped by the ideology of "progress" and productivism, even leading it, in certain cases, without asking too many questions, to the defense of nuclear energy or the automobile industry. However, ecological sensitivity has begun to emerge, notably in the trade unions and left parties of the Nordic countries, Spain, and Germany.

◆ ◆ ◆

The great contribution of ecology has been, and still is, to make us conscious of the dangers threatening the planet as a result of the present mode of production and consumption. The exponential growth of attacks on the environment and the increasing threat of the breakdown of the ecological balance constitute a catastrophic scenario that calls into question the survival of the human species. We are facing a crisis of civilization that demands radical change.

The problem is that the proposals put forward by the leading circles of European political ecology are at best highly inadequate and at worst wholly inappropriate solutions to the ecological crisis. Their main weakness is that they do not acknowledge the necessary connection between productivism and capitalism. Instead, reforms like eco-taxes capable of controlling "excesses" or ideas like "green economics" lead to the illusion of a "clean capitalism." Or, further, taking as a pretext the imitation of Western productivism by bureaucratic command economies, they conceive of capitalism and "socialism" as variants of the same model—an argument that has lost a lot of its attraction after the collapse of so-called "actually existing socialism."

Ecologists are mistaken if they imagine they can do without the Marxian critique of capitalism. An ecology that does not recognize the relation between "productivism" and the logic of profit is destined to fail—or, worse, to become absorbed by the system. Examples abound. The lack of a coherent anticapitalist posture led most of the European green parties—notably in France, Germany, Italy, and Belgium—to become mere "eco-reformist" partners in the social-liberal management of capitalism by center-left governments.

Regarding workers as irremediably devoted to productivism, certain ecologists have avoided the labor movement and have adopted the slogan "neither left nor right." Ex-Marxists converted to ecology hastily say "goodbye to the working class" (André Gorz), while others (Alain Lipietz) insist on the need to abandon "the red"—that is, Marxism or socialism—to join "the green," the new paradigm thought to be the answer to all economic and social problems.

Finally, in so-called fundamentalist or deep-ecology circles, we see, under the pretext of opposing anthropocentrism, a rejection of humanism, which leads to relativist positions that place all living species on the same plane. Should one really maintain that Koch's bacillus or the *Anopheles* mosquito have the same right to life as a child suffering from tuberculosis or malaria?

What, then, is ecosocialism? It is a current of ecological thought and action that appropriates the fundamental gains of Marxism while shaking off its productivist dross. For ecosocialists, the market's profit logic, and the logic of bureaucratic authoritarianism within the late departed "actually existing socialism," are incompatible with the need to safeguard the natural environment. While criticizing the ideology of the dominant sectors of the labor movement, ecosocialists know that the workers and their organizations are an indispensable force for any radical transformation of the system as well as the establishment of a new socialist and ecological society.

Ecosocialism has developed mostly during the last thirty years, thanks to the work of major thinkers like Raymond Williams, Rudolf Bahro (in his earlier writings) and André Gorz (also in his early work), as well as the very useful contributions of James O'Connor, Barry Commoner, John Bellamy Foster, Joel Kovel, Joan Martínez-Alier, Francisco Fernández Buey, Jorge Riechmann (the latter three from Spain), Jean-Paul Deléage, Jean-Marie Harribey (France), Elmar Altvater, Frieder Otto Wolf (Germany), and many others, who publish in journals like *Capitalism Nature Socialism* and *Ecología Política*.

This current is far from politically homogeneous. Still, most of its representatives share certain common themes. Breaking with the productivist ideology of progress—in its capitalist and/or bureaucratic form—and opposed to the infinite expansion of a mode of production and consumption that destroys nature, it represents an original attempt to connect the fundamental ideas of Marxian socialism to the gains of critical ecology.

James O'Connor defines as ecosocialist the theories and movements that seek to subordinate exchange value to use value by organizing production as a function of social needs and the requirements of environmental protection. Their aim, an ecological socialism, would be an ecologically rational society founded on democratic control, social equality, and the predominance of use value. I would add that this conception assumes collective ownership of the means of production, democratic planning that makes it possible for society to define the goals of investment and production, and a new technological structure of the productive forces.

Ecosocialist reasoning rests on two essential arguments:

1. The present mode of production and consumption of advanced capitalist countries, which is based on the logic of boundless accumulation (of capital, profits, and commodities), waste of resources, ostentatious consumption, and the accelerated destruction of the environment, cannot in any way be extended to the whole planet without a major ecological crisis. According to recent calculations, if one extended to the whole world the average energy consumption of the United States, the known reserves of petroleum would be exhausted in nineteen days. Thus, this system necessarily operates on the maintenance and aggravation of the glaring inequality between North and South.

2. Whatever the cause, the continuation of capitalist "progress" and the expansion of a civilization based on a market economy—even under this brutally inequitable form in which the world's majority consume less—directly threatens, in the middle term (any exact forecast would be risky), the very survival of the human species. The protection of the natural environment is thus a humanist imperative.

Rationality limited by the capitalist market, with its shortsighted calculation of profit and loss, stands in intrinsic contradiction to ecological rationality, which takes into account the length of natural cycles. It is not a matter of contrasting "bad" ecocidal capitalists to "good" green capitalists; it is the system itself, based on ruthless competition, the demands of profitability, and the race for rapid profit, which is the destroyer of nature's balance. Would-be green capitalism is nothing but a publicity stunt, a label for the purpose of selling a commodity, or—in the best of cases—a local initiative equivalent to a drop of water on the arid soil of the capitalist desert.

Against commodity fetishism and the reified autonomization of the economy brought about by neoliberalism, the challenge of the future for ecosocialists is the realization of a "moral economy." This moral economy must exist in the sense in which E. P. Thompson used this term, that is, an economic policy founded on nonmonetary and extraeconomic criteria. In other words, it must reintegrate the economic into the ecological, the social, and the political.

Partial reforms are completely inadequate; what is needed is the replacement of the microrationality of profit by a social and ecological macrorationality, which demands a veritable change of civilization. That is impossible without a profound technological reorientation aimed at the replacement of present energy sources by non-polluting and renewable ones, such as wind or solar energy. The first question, therefore, concerns control over the means of production, especially decisions on investment and technological change, which must be taken away from the banks and capitalist enterprises in order to serve society's common good.

Admittedly, radical change concerns not only production but consumption as well. However, the problem of bourgeois/industrial civilization is not—as ecologists often assert—the population's "excessive consumption." Nor is the solution a general "limit" on consumption. It is, rather, the prevalent *type* of consumption, based as it is on ostentation, waste, mercantile alienation, and an accumulationist obsession, that must be called into question.

An economy in transition to socialism, "re-embedded" (as Karl Polanyi would say) in the social and natural environment, would be founded on the democratic choice of priorities and investments by the population itself, not by "the laws of the market" or an omniscient politburo. Local, national, and, sooner or later, international democratic planning would define:

- what products are to be subsidized or even distributed without charge;
- what energy options are to be pursued, even if they are not, in the beginning, the most profitable;
- how to reorganize the transportation system according to social and ecological criteria; and
- what measures to take to repair, as quickly as possible, the enormous environmental damage bequeathed to us by capitalism. And so on . . .

This transition would lead not only to a new mode of production and an egalitarian and democratic society, but also to an alternative mode of life, a new ecosocialist civilization beyond the reign of money, beyond consumption habits artificially produced by advertising, and beyond the unlimited production of commodities such as private automobiles that are harmful to the environment. Utopia? In its etymological sense ("nowhere"), certainly. However, if one does not believe, with Hegel, that "everything that is real is rational, and everything that is rational is real," how does one reflect on substantial rationality without appealing to utopias? Utopia is indispensable to social change, provided it is based on the contradictions found in reality and on real social movements. This is true of ecosocialism, which proposes a strategic alliance between "reds" and "greens"—not in the narrow sense used by politicians applied to social-democratic and green parties, but in the broader sense between the labor movement and the ecological movement—and the movements of solidarity with the oppressed and exploited of the South.

This alliance implies that ecology gives up any tendency to antihumanist naturalism and abandons its claim to have replaced the critique of political economy. From the other side, Marxism needs to overcome its productivism. One way of seeing this would be to discard the mechanistic scheme of the opposition between the forces of production and the relations of production, which impede them. This should be replaced—or at least completed—by the idea that productive forces in the capitalist system become destructive ones. Take, for example, the armament industry or the various branches of production that are destructive of human health and of the natural environment.

◆ ◆ ◆

The revolutionary utopia of green socialism or of solar communism does not imply that one ought not to act right now. Not having illusions about "ecologizing" capitalism does not mean that one cannot join the battle for immediate reforms. For example, certain kinds of eco-taxes could be useful, providing they are based on an egalitarian social logic (make the polluters pay, not the public) and that one disposes of the economic-calculation myth of a "market price" for ecological damages, which are incommensurate with any monetary point of view. We desperately need to win time, to struggle immediately for the banning of the hydrochlorofluorocarbons (HCFCs) that are destroying the ozone layer, for a moratorium on genetically modified organisms, for severe limitations on the emissions of greenhouse gases, and to privilege public transportation over the polluting and antisocial private automobile.

The trap awaiting us here is the formal acknowledgment of our demands, which empties them of content. An exemplary case is that of the Kyoto Protocol on climate change, which provides for a minimal reduction of 5 percent of gases responsible for global warming in relation to 1990—certainly too little to achieve any results. As is known, the United States, the main power responsible for the emission of these gases, has stubbornly refused to sign the protocol. As for Europe, Japan, and Canada, they have signed the protocol while adding clauses such as the famous "market of rights of emission," which enormously restrict the treaty's already limited reach. Rather than the long-term interests of humanity, it is the short-term view of the oil multinationals and the automobile industry that has predominated.

The struggle for ecosocial reforms can be the vehicle for dynamic change, a "transition" between minimal demands and the maximal program, provided one rejects the pressure and arguments of the ruling interests for "competitiveness" and "modernization" in the name of the "rules of the market."

Certain immediate demands have already, or could rapidly, become the locus of a convergence between social and ecological movements, trade unions and defenders of the environment, "reds" and "greens," such as:

- promoting inexpensive or free public transportation—trains, metros, buses, trams—as an alternative to the choking and pollution of cities and countrysides by private automobiles and the trucking system;
- rejecting the system of debt and extreme neoliberal "structural adjustments" imposed by the International Monetary Fund and the World Bank on the countries of the South, with dramatic social and ecological consequences: massive unemployment, destruction of social protections, and destruction of natural resources through export;
- defending public health against the pollution of the air, water, and food due to the greed of large capitalist enterprises; and
- reducing work time to cope with unemployment and create a society that privileges free time over the accumulation of goods.

All of the emancipatory social movements must be brought together to birth a new civilization that is more humane and respectful of nature. As Jorge Riechmann says so aptly: "This project cannot reject any of the colors of the rainbow—neither the red of the anti-capitalist and egalitarian labor movement, nor the violet of the struggles for women's liberation, nor the white of non-violent movements for peace, nor the anti-authoritarian black of the libertarians and anarchists, and even less the green of the struggle for a just and free humanity on a habitable planet."

Radical political ecology has become a social and political force present on the terrain of most European countries and also, to a certain extent, in the United States. However, nothing would be more wrong than to regard ecological questions as only of concern to the countries of the North—a luxury of rich societies. Increasingly, social movements with an ecological dimension are developing in the countries of peripheral capitalism—the South.

These movements are reacting to a growing aggravation of the ecological problems of Asia, Africa, and Latin America that result from a deliberate policy of "pollution export" by the imperialist countries. The economic "legitimation"—from the point of view of the capitalist market economy—was bluntly articulated in an internal World Bank memo by the institution's chief economist, Lawrence Summers (the president of Harvard University), published in the *Economist* in early 1992. Summers said:

> Just between you and me, shouldn't the World Bank be encouraging more migration of dirty industries to the LDCs [less developed countries]? I can think of three reasons: 1) The measurement of the costs of health-impairing pollution depends

on the forgone earnings from increased morbidity and mortality. From this point of view a given amount of health-impairing pollution should be done in the country with the lowest cost, which will be the country with the lowest wages. I think the economic logic behind dumping a load of toxic waste in the lowest wage country is impeccable, and we should face up to that. 2) The costs of pollution are likely to be non-linear as the initial increments of pollution probably have very low costs. I've always thought that under-populated countries in Africa are vastly under-polluted; their air quality is probably vastly inefficiently low compared to Los Angeles or Mexico City. . . . 3) The demand for a clean environment for aesthetic and health reasons is likely to have very high income-elasticity. The concern over an agent that causes a one in a million change in the odds of prostate cancer is obviously going to be much higher in a country where people survive to get prostate cancer than in a country where under-five mortality is 200 per thousand.[1]

In this statement we see a cynical formulation that clearly reveals the logic of global capital—in contrast to all the mollifying speeches on "development" produced by the international financial institutions.

In the countries of the South, we thus see the birth of movements which Joan Martínez-Alier calls "the ecology of the poor" or even "ecological neo-Narodnism." These include popular mobilizations in defense of peasant agriculture and communal access to natural resources threatened with destruction by the aggressive expansion of the market (or the state), as well as struggles against the degradation of the local environment caused by unequal exchange, dependent industrialization, genetic modifications, and the development of capitalism (agribusiness) in the countrysides. Often these movements do not define themselves as ecological, but their struggle nevertheless has a crucial ecological dimension.

It goes without saying that these movements are not against the improvements brought by technological progress; on the contrary, the demand for electricity, running water, sewage, and more medical dispensaries are prominent in their platforms. What they reject is the pollution and destruction of their natural surroundings in the name of "market laws" and the imperatives of capitalist "expansion." A recent article by the Peruvian peasant leader Hugo Blanco is a striking articulation of the meaning of this "ecology of the poor":

> At first sight, the defenders of the environment or the conserva-tionists appear as nice people, slightly crazy, whose principal aim in life is to prevent the disappearance of blue whales and panda bears. The common people have more important things occupy-ing them, for example how to get their daily bread. However, there are in Peru a great many people who are defenders of the environ-ment. To be sure, if one told them "you are ecologists," they would probably reply "ecologist my eye." And yet, in their struggle against the pollution caused by the Southern Peru Copper Cor-poration, are not the inhabitants of the town of Ilo and the sur-rounding villages defenders of the environment? And is not the population of the Amazon completely ecologist, ready to die to defend their forests against pillage? The same goes for the poor population of Lima, when they protest against water pollution.
>
> Among the innumerable manifestations of the "ecology of the poor," one movement is particularly exemplary by its breadth, which is at once social and ecological, local and global, "red" and "green": the struggle of Chico Mendes and the Forest Peoples Al-liance (Aliança dos Povos da Floresta) in defense of the Brazilian Amazon against the destructive activity of the large landowners and multinational agribusiness.

Let us briefly recall the main aspects of this confrontation. In the early 1980s, a militant trade unionist linked to the Unified Workers' Confederation (Central Única dos Trabalhadores, CUT) and partisan of the new socialist movement represented by the Brazilian Workers Party, Chico Mendes organized occupations of land by peasants who earned their livelihoods from rubber tapping (*seringueiros*) against the *latifundistas* who bulldozed the forest in order to establish pasture lands. Later Mendes succeeded in bringing together peasants, agricultural workers, seringueiros, trade unionists, and Indigenous tribes—with the support of the church's base communities—to form the Forest Peoples Alliance, which blocked many attempts at deforestation. The international outcry resulting from these actions earned him the United Nations Global 500 Award in 1987, but shortly afterward, in December 1988, the latifundistas made him pay dearly for his struggle by having him killed by paid assassins.

Through its linking of socialism and ecology, peasant and Indigenous struggles, survival of local populations and taking responsibility for a global concern (the protection of the last great tropical rainforest), this movement can become a paradigm for future popular mobilizations in the South.

◆ ◆ ◆

Today, at the turn of the twentieth century, radical political ecology has become one of the most important ingredients of the vast movement against capitalist neoliberal globalization, which is developing in the North as well as the South. The massive presence of ecologists was one of the striking aspects of the big demonstration in Seattle against the World Trade Organization in 1999. And at the World Social Forum in Porto Alegre in 2001, one of the most powerful symbolic acts of the event was the operation led by activists of the Landless Workers' Movement (Movimento dos Trabalhadores Rurais Sem Terra) and José Bové's French Farmers' Confederation (Confederation Paysanne): digging up a field of Monsanto's genetically modified corn. The battle against the uncontrolled spread of genetically modified food is mobilizing in Brazil, France, and other countries. This struggle brings together not only the ecological movement but also the farmers' movement, parts of the left, and members of the general public who are disturbed by the unforeseeable consequences of genetic modification on public health and the natural environment. The struggle against the commodification of the world and the defense of the environment, resistance to the dictatorship of multinationals, and the battle for ecology are intimately linked in the reflection and praxis of the world movement against capitalist/liberal globalization.

CHAPTER TWO

Ecosocialism and Democratic Planning

If capitalism can't be reformed to subordinate profit to human survival, what alternative is there but to move to some sort of nationally and globally planned economy? Problems like climate change require the "visible hand" of direct planning. . . . Our capitalist corporate leaders can't help themselves, have no choice but to systematically make wrong, irrational, and ultimately— given the technology they command—globally suicidal decisions about the economy and the environment. So then, what other choice do we have than to consider a true ecosocialist alternative?
—Richard Smith[2]

Ecosocialism is an attempt to provide a radical civilizational alternative to what Marx called capitalism's "destructive progress."[3] It advances an economic policy founded on the nonmonetary and extraeconomic criteria of social needs and ecological equilibrium. Grounded on the basic arguments of the ecological movement and of the Marxist critique of political economy, this dialectical synthesis—attempted by a broad spectrum of authors, from André Gorz (in his early writings) to Elmar Altvater, James O'Connor, Joel Kovel, and John Bellamy Foster—is at the same time a critique of "market ecology," which does not challenge the capitalist system, and of "productivist socialism," which ignores the issue of natural limits.

According to O'Connor, the aim of ecological socialism is a new society based on ecological rationality, democratic control, social equality, and the predominance of use value over exchange value.[4] I would add that these aims require: (a) collective ownership of the means of production ("collective" here meaning public, cooperative, or communitarian property); (b) democratic planning, which makes it possible for society to define the goals of investment and production, and (c) a new technological structure of the productive forces. In other words, a revolutionary social and economic transformation.[5]

For ecosocialists, the problem with the main currents of political ecology, represented by most green parties, is that they do not seem to take into account the intrinsic contradiction between the capitalist dynamics of the unlimited expansion of capital and accumulation of profits and the preservation of the environment. This leads to a critique of productivism, which is often relevant but does not lead beyond an ecologically reformed "market economy." The result has been that many green parties have become the ecological alibi of center-left social-liberal governments.[6]

On the other hand, the problem with the dominant trends of the left during the twentieth century—social democracy and the Soviet-inspired Communist movement—is their acceptance of the actually existing pattern of productive forces. While the former limited themselves to a reformed—at best Keynesian—version of the capitalist system, the latter developed an authoritarian collectivist—or state capitalist—form of productivism. In both cases, environmental issues remained out of sight or were at least marginalized.

Marx and Engels themselves were not unaware of the environmentally destructive consequences of the capitalist mode of production; there are several passages in *Capital* and other writings that point to this understanding.[7] Moreover, they believed that the aim of socialism is not to produce more and more commodities, but to give human beings free time to fully develop their potentialities. To this extent they have little in common with "productivism," i.e., with the idea that the unlimited expansion of production is an aim in itself.

However, the passages in their writings to the effect that socialism will permit the development of productive forces beyond the limits imposed on them by the capitalist system imply that socialist transformation concerns only the capitalist relations of production, which have become an obstacle ("chains" is the term often used) to the free development of the existing productive forces. Socialism would mean above all the social appropriation of these productive capacities, putting them at the service of the workers. To quote a passage from *Anti-Dühring*, a canonical work for many generations of Marxists, under socialism "society takes possession openly and without detours of the productive forces that have become too large" for the existing system.[8]

The experience of the Soviet Union illustrates the problems that result from such a collectivist appropriation of the capitalist productive apparatus. From the beginning, the thesis of the socialization of the existing productive forces predominated. It is true that during the first years after the October Revolution an ecological current was able to develop, and the Soviet authorities took certain limited environmental protection measures. But with the process of Stalinist bureaucratization, productivist methods both in industry and agriculture were imposed by totalitarian means while ecologists were marginalized or eliminated. The catastrophe of Chernobyl was the ultimate example of the disastrous consequences of this imitation of Western productive technologies. A change in the forms of property that is not followed by democratic management and a reorganization of the productive system can only lead to a dead end.

A critique of the productivist ideology of "progress" and of the idea of a "socialist" exploitation of nature had appeared already in the writings of some dissident Marxists of the 1930s, such as Walter Benjamin. But it is mainly during the last few decades that ecosocialism has developed as a challenge to the thesis of the neutrality of productive forces, which predominated in the main tendencies of the left during the twentieth century.

Ecosocialists should take their inspiration from Marx's remarks on the Paris Commune: Workers cannot take possession of the capitalist state apparatus and put it to work at their service. They have to "break it" and replace it with a radically different, democratic, and nonstatist form of political power. The same applies, mutatis mutandis, to the productive apparatus, which is not "neutral" but carries in its structure the imprint of its development at the service of capital accumulation and the unlimited expansion of the market. This puts it in contradiction with the needs of environmental protection and with the health of the population. One must therefore "revolutionize" it in a process of radical transformation.

Of course many scientific and technological achievements of modernity are precious, but the whole productive system must be transformed, and this can be done only by ecosocialist methods: i.e., through a democratic planning of the economy that takes into account the preservation of the ecological equilibrium. This may mean discontinuing certain branches of production: for instance, nuclear plants, certain methods of mass/industrial fishing (which are responsible for the near-extermination of several species in the seas), the destructive logging of tropical forests, etc.—the list is very long. It first of all requires, however, a revolution in the energy system, with the replacement of the present sources (essentially fossil) that are responsible for the pollution and poisoning of the environment with renewable sources of energy: water, wind, sun. The issue of energy is decisive because fossil energy (oil, coal) is responsible for much of the planet's pollution as well as for the disastrous climate change. Nuclear energy is a false alternative not only because of the danger of new Chernobyls, but also because nobody knows what to do with the thousands of tons of radioactive waste—toxic for hundreds, thousands, and in some cases millions of years—and the gigantic carcasses of contaminated obsolete plants. Solar energy, which has never aroused much interest in capitalist societies (not being "profitable" or "competitive"), must become the object of intensive research and development and play a key role in the building of an alternative energy system.

All this must be accomplished under the necessary condition of full and equitable employment. This condition is essential not only to meet the requirement of social justice, but in order to ensure working-class support for the process of structurally transforming the productive forces. This process is impossible without public control over the means of production and over planning—that is, public decisions on investment and technological change, which must be taken away from the banks and capitalist enterprises in order to serve society's common good.

But putting these decisions into the hands of workers is not enough. In volume 3 of *Capital,* Marx defined socialism as a society where "the associated producers rationally organize their exchange (*Stoffwechsel*) with nature." But in volume 1 of *Capital* there is a broader approach: socialism is conceived as "an association of free human beings (*Menschen*), which works with common (*gemein-schaftlichen*) means of production."[9] This is a much more appropriate conception: the rational organization of production and consumption has to be the work not only of the "producers," but also of the consumers, in fact of the whole society, with its productive and "nonproductive" population, which includes students, youth, housewives (and househusbands), pensioners, and so on.

The whole society in this sense will be able to choose, democratically, which productive lines are to be privileged and how many resources are to be invested in education, health, or culture.[10] The prices of goods themselves would not be left to the laws of supply and demand but determined as far as possible according to social, political, and ecological criteria. Initially, this might only involve taxes on certain products and subsidized prices for others, but ideally, as the transition to socialism moves forward, more and more products and services would be distributed free of charge according to the will of the citizens.

Far from being "despotic" in itself, democratic planning is the exercise by a whole society of its freedom of decision. This is what is required for liberation from the alienating and reified "economic laws" and "iron cages" of capitalist and bureaucratic structures. Democratic planning combined with the reduction of labor time would be a decisive step of humanity toward what Marx called "the kingdom of freedom." This is because a significant increase in free time is in fact a condition for working people's participation in the democratic discussion and management of the economy and society.

Partisans of the free market point to the failure of Soviet planning as a reason to reject, out of hand, any idea of an organized economy. Without entering the discussion on the achievements and miseries of the Soviet experience, it was obviously a form of dictatorship over needs, to use the expression of György Márkus and his friends in the Budapest School: a nondemocratic and authoritarian system that gave a monopoly over all decisions to a small oligarchy of techno-bureaucrats. It was not planning itself that led to dictatorship, but the growing limitations on democracy in the Soviet state and, after Lenin's death, the establishment of a totalitarian bureaucratic power, which led to an increasingly undemocratic and authoritarian system of planning. If socialism is defined as control by the workers and the population in general over the process of production, the Soviet Union under Stalin and his successors was a far cry from it.

The failure of the USSR illustrates the limits and contradictions of bureaucratic planning, which is inevitably inefficient and arbitrary: it cannot be used as an argument against democratic planning.[11] The socialist conception of planning is nothing other than the radical democratization of economy: If political decisions are not to be left to a small elite of rulers, why should not the same principle apply to economic decisions? The issue of the specific balance to be struck between planning and market mechanisms is admittedly a difficult one: during the first stages of a new society markets will certainly retain an important place, but as the transition to socialism advances planning will become more and more predominant, as against the laws of exchange value.[12]

Engels insisted that a socialist society "will have to establish a plan of production taking into account the means of production, specially including the labour force. It will be, in last instance, the useful effects of various use-objects, compared between themselves and in relation to the quantity of labour necessary for their production, that will determine the plan."[13] In capitalism, use value is only a means—often a trick—at the service of exchange value and profit (which explains, by the way, why so many products in the present-day society are substantially useless). In a planned socialist economy use value is the only criterion for the production of goods and services, with far-reaching economic, social, and ecological consequences. As Joel Kovel has observed: "The enhancement of use-values and the corresponding restructuring of needs becomes now the social regulator of technology rather than, as under capital, the conversion of time into surplus value and money."[14]

In the type of democratic planning system envisaged here, the plan concerns the main economic options, not the administration of local restaurants, groceries and bakeries, small shops, and artisan enterprises or services. It is important to emphasize, as well, that planning is not in contradiction with workers' self-management of their productive units. While the decision, made through the planning system, to transform, say, an auto plant into one producing buses and trams would be made by society as a whole, the internal organization and functioning of the plant should be democratically managed by its own workers. There has been much discussion of the "centralized" or "decentralized" character of planning, but it could be argued that the real issue is democratic control of the plan at all levels: local, regional, national, continental, and, hopefully, international, since ecological issues such as global warming are planetary and can be dealt with only on a global scale. One could call this proposition global democratic planning. Even at this level, it would be quite the opposite of what is usually described as "central planning," since the economic and social decisions are not made by any "center" but democratically decided by the populations concerned.

Of course, there will inevitably be tensions and contradictions between self-managed establishments or local democratic administrations and broader social groups. Negotiation mechanisms can help to solve many such conflicts, but ultimately the broadest groups of those concerned, if they are the majority, have the right to impose their views. To give an example: a self-administered factory decides to evacuate its toxic waste into a river. The population of a whole region is in danger of being polluted: it can therefore, after a democratic debate, decide that production in this unit must be discontinued until a satisfactory solution is found to control its waste. Hopefully, in an ecosocialist society, the factory workers themselves will have enough ecological consciousness to avoid making decisions that are dangerous to the environment and the health of the local population. But instituting means of ensuring that the broadest social interests have the decisive say, as the above example suggests, does not mean that issues concerning internal management are not to be vested at the level of the factory, school, neighborhood, hospital, or town.

Socialist planning must be grounded on a democratic and pluralist debate at all the levels where decisions are to be made. As organized in the form of parties, platforms, or any other political movements, delegates to planning bodies must be elected and different propositions submitted to all the people concerned with them. That is, representative democracy must be completed, and corrected, by direct democracy, where people directly choose—at the local, national, and later global level—between major options. Should public transportation be free? Should the owners of private cars pay special taxes to subsidize public transportation? Should solar energy be subsidized, in order to compete with fossil energy? Should the work week be reduced to thirty or twenty hours, or fewer, even if this means reducing production? The democratic nature of planning is not incompatible with the existence of experts: their role is not to decide but to present their views—often different, if not opposite—to the democratic process of decision making. As Ernest Mandel put it: "Governments, parties, planning boards, scientists, technocrats or whoever can make suggestions, put forward proposals, try to influence people. . . . But under a multi-party system, such proposals will never be unanimous: people will have the choice between coherent alternatives. And the right and power to decide should be in the hands of the majority of producers/consumers/citizens, not of anybody else. What is paternalistic or despotic about that?"[15]

What guarantee is there that the people will make the right ecological choices, even at the price of giving up some of their habits of consumption? There is no such "guarantee," other than the reasonable expectation that the rationality of democratic decisions will prevail once the power of commodity fetishism is broken. Of course, errors will be committed by popular choices, but who believes that experts make no errors themselves? One cannot imagine the establishment of such a new society without the majority of the population having achieved, by their struggles, their self-education, and their social experience, a high level of socialist/ecological consciousness, and this makes it reasonable to suppose that serious errors—including decisions which are inconsistent with environmental needs—will be corrected.[16] In any case, are not the alternatives—the blind market, or an ecological dictatorship of "experts"—much more dangerous than the democratic process, with all its limitations?

It is true that planning requires the existence of executive/technical bodies in charge of putting into practice what has been decided, but they are not necessarily authoritarian if they are under permanent democratic control from below and include workers' self-management in a process of democratic administration. Of course, one cannot expect the majority of the people to spend all their free time in self-management or participatory meetings; as Ernest Mandel remarked, "Self-administration does not entail the disappearance of delegation. It combines decision-making by the citizens with stricter control of delegates by their respective electorate."[17]

Michael Albert's "participatory economy" (parecon) has been the object of some debate in the global justice movement. Although there are some serious shortcomings in his overall approach, which seems to ignore ecology and counterposes parecon to "socialism" as understood in the bureaucratic/centralized Soviet model, nevertheless parecon has some common features with the kind of ecosocialist planning proposed here: opposition to the capitalist market and to bureaucratic planning; a reliance on workers' self-organization; antiauthoritarianism. Albert's model of participatory planning is based on a complex institutional construction:

> The participants in participatory planning are the workers' councils and federations, the consumers' councils and federations, and various Iteration Facilitation Boards (IFBs). Conceptually, the

planning procedure is quite simple. An IFB announces what we call "indicative prices" for all goods, resources, categories of labour, and capital. Consumers' councils and federations respond with consumption proposals taking the indicative prices of final goods and services as estimates of the social cost of providing them. Workers' councils and federations respond with production proposals listing the outputs they would make available and the inputs they would need to produce them, again, taking the indicative prices as estimates of the social benefits of outputs and true opportunity costs of inputs. An IFB then calculates the excess demand or supply for each good and adjusts the indicative price for the good up, or down, in light of the excess demand or supply, and in accord with socially agreed algorithms. Using the new indicative prices, consumers' and workers' councils and federations revise and resubmit their proposals. . . . In place of rule over workers by capitalists or by coordinators, parecon is an economy in which workers and consumers together cooperatively determine their economic options and benefit from them in ways fostering equity, solidarity, diversity, and self-management.[18]

The main problem with this conception—which, by the way, is not "quite simple" but extremely elaborate and sometimes quite obscure—is that it seems to reduce "planning" to a sort of negotiation between producers and consumers on the issue of prices, inputs and outputs, supply and demand. For instance, the branch workers' council of the automobile industry would meet with the council of consumers to discuss prices and to adapt supply to demand. What this leaves out is precisely what constitutes the main issue in ecosocialist planning: a reorganization of the transport system, radically reducing the place of the private car. Since ecosocialism requires entire sectors of industry to disappear—nuclear plants, for instance—

and massive investment in small or almost nonexistent sectors (such as solar energy), how can this be dealt with by "cooperative negotiations" between the existing units of production and consumer councils on "inputs" and "indicative prices"? Albert's model mirrors the existing technological and productive structure, and is too "economistic" to take into account the global, sociopolitical, and socioecological interests of the population—the interests of individuals, as citizens and as human beings, which cannot be reduced to their economic interests as producers and consumers. He leaves out not only the state as an institution—a respectable option—but also politics as the confrontation of different economic, social, political, ecological, cultural, and civilizational options, locally, nationally, and globally.

This is very important because the passage from capitalist "destructive progress" to socialism is a historical process, a permanent revolutionary transformation of society, culture, and mentalities—and politics, in the sense just defined, cannot but be central to this process. It is important to emphasize that such a process cannot begin without a revolutionary transformation of social and political structures, and the vast majority of the population's active support of an ecosocialist program. The development of socialist consciousness and ecological awareness is a process in which the decisive factor is people's own collective experience of struggle, moving from local and partial confrontations to the radical change of society.

Some ecologists believe that the only alternative to productivism is to stop growth altogether, or to replace it by negative growth—what the French call *décroissance*—and drastically reduce the population's excessively high level of consumption by cutting energy expenditure by half through renouncing individual family houses, central heating, and washing machines, and so on. Since these and similar measures of draconian austerity risk being quite unpopular, some of the advocates of *décroissance* play with the idea of a sort of "ecological dictatorship."[19] Against such pessimistic views, socialist optimists believe that technical progress and the use of renewable sources of energy will permit unlimited growth and abundance, so that all can receive "according to their needs."

It seems to me that both these schools share a purely quantitative conception of "growth"—positive or negative—and of the development of productive forces. There is a third position, however, which seems to me more appropriate: a qualitative transformation of development. This means putting an end to capitalism's monstrous waste of resources based on the large-scale production of useless and harmful products. The armaments industry is a good example, but a great part of the "goods" produced under capitalism—with their built-in obsolescence—have no other use but to generate profit for big corporations. The issue is not "excessive consumption" in the abstract, but the prevalent type of consumption, based as it is on conspicuous consumption, massive waste, mercantile alienation, obsessive accumulation of goods, and the compulsive acquisition of pseudo-novelties imposed by "fashion." A new society would orient production toward satisfying authentic needs, beginning with those which could be described as "biblical"—water, food, clothing, housing—but including also basic services such as health, education, transportation, and culture.

Obviously, the countries of the global South, where these needs are very far from being satisfied, will need a much higher level of "development"—building railroads, hospitals, sewage systems, and other infrastructures—than the advanced industrial ones. But there is no reason why this cannot be accomplished with a productive system that is environmentally friendly and based on renewable energies. These countries will need to produce large amounts of food to nourish their hungry populations, but this can be much better achieved—as the peasant movements organized worldwide in the Via Campesina network have been arguing for years—through peasant biological agriculture based on family units, cooperatives, or collectivist farms than through the destructive and antisocial methods of industrialized agribusiness, based on the intensive use of pesticides, chemicals, and GMOs. Instead of the present monstrous debt system and the imperialist exploitation of the resources of the South by the industrial/capitalist countries, there would be a flow of technical and economic help from the North to the South, without the need—as some puritan and ascetic ecologists seem to believe—for the population in Europe and North America to reduce their standard of living in absolute terms. Instead, they would only get rid of the obsessive consumption induced by the capitalist system of useless commodities that do not correspond to any real need, while redefining the meaning of standard of living to connote a way of life that is actually richer, while consuming less.

How to distinguish the authentic from artificial, false, and makeshift needs? The advertising industry—which induces needs through mental manipulation—has invaded all spheres of human life in modern capitalist societies: not only nourishment and clothing, but sports, culture, religion, and politics are shaped according to its rules. It has invaded our streets, mailboxes, TV screens, newspapers, and landscapes in a permanent, aggressive, and insidious way, and it decisively contributes to habits of conspicuous and compulsive consumption. Moreover, it wastes an astronomic amount of oil, electricity, labor time, paper, chemicals, and other raw materials—all paid for by consumers—in a branch of "production" that is not only useless, from a human viewpoint, but directly opposed to real social needs. While advertising is an indispensable dimension of a capitalist market economy, it would have no place in a society in transition to socialism, where it would be replaced by information on goods and services provided by consumer associations. The criterion for distinguishing an authentic need from an artificial one would be its persistence after the suppression of advertising. Of course, for some time old habits of consumption would persist, and nobody has the right to tell the people what their needs are. Changing patterns of consumption is a historical process as well as an educational challenge.

Some commodities, such as the individual car, raise more complex problems. Private cars are a public nuisance, killing and maiming hundreds of thousands of people yearly on a world scale, polluting the air in large cities—with dire consequences for the health of children and older people—and significantly contributing to climate change. However, they fulfill real needs under the present-day conditions of capitalism. Local experiments in some European towns with ecologically minded administrations show that it is possible—and approved by the majority of the population—to progressively limit the role of the individual automobile in favor of buses and trams. In a process of transition to ecosocialism, where public transportation—above or underground—would be vastly extended and free of charge and where pedestrians would have protected lanes, the private car would play a much smaller role than in bourgeois society, where it has become a fetish promoted by insistent and aggressive advertisement, a prestige symbol, an identity sign (in the United States, the driver's license is the recognized ID), and a focus of personal, social, and erotic life.[20] It will be much easier, in the transition to a new society, to drastically reduce the transportation of goods by trucks—responsible for terrible accidents and high levels of pollution—replacing them with rail transport or what the French call *ferroutage* (trucks transported in trains from one town to another): only the absurd logic of capitalist "competition" explains the dangerous growth of the trucking system.

Yes, the pessimists will answer, but individuals are moved by infinite aspirations and desires that have to be controlled, checked, contained, and if necessary repressed, and this may call for some limitations on democracy. But ecosocialism is based on a reasonable expectation, which Marx already held: the predominance, in a society without classes and liberated of capitalist alienation, of "being" over "having," i.e., of free time for the personal accomplishment by cultural, sportive, playful, scientific, erotic, artistic, and political activities, rather than the desire for an infinite possession of products. Compulsive acquisitiveness is induced by the commodity fetishism inherent in the capitalist system, by the dominant ideology and by advertising: nothing proves that it is part of an "eternal human nature." As Ernest Mandel emphasized, "The continual accumulation of more and more goods (with declining 'marginal utility') is by no means a universal and even predominant feature of human behavior. The development of talents and inclinations for their own sake; the protection of health and life; care for children; the development of rich social relations . . . all these become major motivations once basic material needs have been satisfied."[21]

As we have insisted, this does not mean that conflicts will not arise, particularly during the transition process between the requirements of environmental protection and social needs, between ecological imperatives and the necessity of developing basic infrastructures, particularly in poor countries, and between popular consumer habits and the scarcity of resources. A classless society is not a society without contradictions and conflicts. These are inevitable: it will be the task of democratic planning, in an ecosocialist perspective liberated from the imperatives of capital and profit, to solve them through pluralist and open discussion, leading to society itself making decisions. Such a grassroots and participative democracy is the only way, not to avoid errors, but to permit the social collectivity to correct its own mistakes.

Is this a utopia? In its etymological sense—"something that exists nowhere"—certainly. But are not utopias (that is, visions of an alternative future), wish-images of a different society, a necessary feature of any movement that wants to challenge the established order? As Daniel Singer explained in his literary and political testament *Whose Millennium?*, in a powerful chapter entitled "Realistic Utopia,"

> If the establishment now looks so solid, despite the circumstances, and if the labor movement or the broader left are so crippled, so paralyzed, it is because of the failure to offer a radical alternative. . . . The basic principle of the game is that you question neither the fundamentals of the argument nor the foundations of society. Only a global alternative, breaking with these rules of resignation and surrender, can give the movement of emancipation genuine scope.[22]

The socialist and ecological utopia is only an objective possibility, not the inevitable result of the contradictions of capitalism or the "iron laws of history." One cannot predict the future, except in conditional terms; what is predictable is that in the absence of an ecosocialist transformation, of a radical change in the civilizational paradigm, the logic of capitalism will lead to dramatic ecological disasters, threatening the health and the lives of millions of human beings and perhaps even the survival of our species.

To dream and to struggle for a green socialism, or, as some say, a solar communism, does not mean that one does not fight for concrete and urgent reforms. Without any illusions about a "clean capitalism," one must try to win time and to impose on the powers that be some elementary changes: banning the HCFCs that are destroying the ozone layer, a general moratorium on genetically modified organisms, a drastic reduction in the emission of greenhouse gases, strict regulation of the fishing industry as well as of the use of pesticides and chemicals in agro-industrial production, taxing polluting cars, developing public transportation on a much greater scale, progressively replacing trucks with trains. These and similar issues are at the heart of the agenda of the global justice movement and the World Social Forums. This is an important new political development that has permitted, since Seattle in 1999, the convergence of social and environmental movements in a common struggle against the system.

These urgent ecosocial demands can lead to a process of radicalization, if such demands are not adapted so as to fit in with the requirements of "competitiveness." According to the logic of what Marxists call "a transitional program," each small victory, each partial advance, leads immediately to a higher demand, a more radical aim. Such struggles around concrete issues are important not only because partial victories are welcome in themselves, but also because they contribute to raise ecological and socialist consciousness and promote activity and self-organization from below: both would be necessary and indeed decisive preconditions for a radical, that is, revolutionary, transformation of the world.

Local experiments such as car-free areas in several European towns, organic agricultural cooperatives launched by the Brazilian peasant movement (MST), or the participative budget in Porto Alegre and, for a few years, in the Brazilian state of Rio Grande do Sul (under Workers' Party, or Partido dos Trabalhadores, governor Olívio Dutra), are limited but interesting examples of social/ecological change. By permitting local assemblies to decide budget priorities, Porto Alegre became—until the left lost the 2002 municipal election—perhaps the most attractive example of "planning from below," in spite of its limitations.[23] It must be admitted, however, that even if some national governments have taken a few progressive measures, on the whole the experience of left-center or left-green coalitions in Europe or Latin America has been rather disappointing, remaining firmly inside the limits of a social-liberal policy of adaptation to capitalist globalization. There will be no radical transformation unless the forces committed to a radical socialist and ecological program become hegemonic, in the Gramscian sense of the word. In one sense, time is on our side as we work for change, because the global situation of the environment is becoming worse and worse and the threats are coming closer and closer. But on the other hand, time is running out, because in some years—no one can say how many—the damage may be irreversible. There is no reason for optimism: the entrenched ruling elites of the system are incredibly powerful and the forces of radical opposition are still small. But they are the only hope that capitalism's "destructive progress" will be halted. Walter Benjamin defined revolutions as being not the locomotives of history, but humanity reaching for the train's emergency brakes before it falls into the abyss.[24]

CHAPTER THREE

Ecology and Advertising

Climate change has brought the global environmental crisis to its crux. The primary point that must be noted is that the pace of climate change is accelerating much more rapidly than had been forecast. Accumulation of carbon dioxide, rising temperatures, melting polar ice caps, and "eternal snows," droughts, floods: all are speeding up, and previous scientific analyses, their ink scarcely dry, turn out to have been too optimistic. More and more, in projections for the next one, two, or three decades, the highest estimates are becoming accepted minima. And to that must be added the all-too-little-studied amplifying factors that today pose the risk of a qualitative leap in the greenhouse effect, leading to runaway global warming.

There are still some 400 billion tons of carbon dioxide confined in the permafrost, that frozen tundra that extends through Canada and Siberia. But how can the glaciers melt without the permafrost melting too? There are few depictions of the worst-case scenario, in which global temperatures rise by five to six degrees Celsius: scientists steer clear of painting catastrophic pictures. But we already know what looms: rising sea levels flooding not only Dhaka and other Asian coastal cities, but also London, Amsterdam, Venice, New York; desertification on an enormous scale; shortages of drinking water; repeated natural catastrophes. The list goes on. At a temperature six degrees higher, it becomes questionable whether the planet will still be habitable for our species. We have, alas, no other planet to which to move.

Who is responsible for this situation, unheard of in human history? Scientists answer—humans. A true answer, but a bit incomplete. Humans have lived on earth for many millennia, but atmospheric carbon dioxide levels became dangerous only a few decades ago. In reality, the fault lies with the capitalist system: its absurd and irrational logic of unlimited expansion and capital accumulation, its obsessive drive to increase material production in pursuit of profits.

The narrow-minded rationality of the capitalist market, with its short-term calculus of profit and loss, is intrinsically contradictory to the rationality of the living environment, which operates in terms of long natural cycles. It is not that "bad" ecocidal capitalists stand in the way of "good" green capitalists. It is the system itself, based on pitiless competition, demand for return on investment, and the search for quick profits, that is the destroyer of ecological equilibrium.

In contradistinction to the fetishism of commodity production and the automatically self-adjusting economy propounded by neoliberal economics, what is at stake is the emergence of a "moral economics"—economic policies based on nonmonetary and extraeconomic criteria, as E. P. Thompson suggested: in other words, the reintegration of economics into its environmental, social, and political integument. Partial reforms are totally insufficient. What is needed is to replace the microrationality of the profitability criterion with an environmental and social macrorationality, which means that civilization will have to operate according to a different paradigm. This is impossible without a thoroughgoing transformation of technology aimed at replacing current energy sources with non-polluting and renewable sources such as direct solar and wind energy. The first question demanding an answer is, therefore, that of control over the means of production and, above all, over decisions on investment and choice of technologies, which must be seized from banks and other corporations and made a function of the common good.

Of course, radical change involves consumption as well as production. Nevertheless, the problem of industrial capitalist civilization is not—as some environmentalists often claim—"excessive consumption" by the masses, and the solution is not a general "limitation" of consumption, not even in the advanced capitalist countries. The problem is the prevailing type of consumption based on "false needs": display, waste, commodity fetishism. What is needed is production aimed at satisfying genuine needs, beginning with those that might be called basic: food, water, shelter, garments.

How can these real needs be distinguished from their artificial and meretricious counterparts? By the fact that the latter are produced by the system of mental manipulation called "advertising." Contrary to the claim of free-market ideology, supply is not a response to demand. Capitalist firms usually create the demand for their products by various marketing techniques, advertising tricks, and planned obsolescence. Advertising plays an essential role in the production of consumerist demand by inventing false "needs" and stimulating the formation of compulsive consumption habits, totally violating the conditions for maintaining planetary ecological equilibrium. The criterion by which an authentic need is to be distinguished from an artificial one is whether it can be expected to persist without the benefit of advertising. How long would the consumption of Coca-Cola or Pepsi-Cola go on if the persistent advertising campaigns for those products were terminated? Such examples could be indefinitely multiplied.

"Of course," pessimists will reply, "but individuals are motivated by an infinity of desires and aspirations, and it is these that will have to be controlled and repressed." Well, the hope for a paradigmatic change in civilization is indeed based on a wager, as propounded by Karl Marx, that in a society freed from capitalism "being" will be valued over "having." Personal fulfillment will be achieved through cultural, athletic, erotic, political, artistic, and playful activities, rather than through the unlimited accumulation of property and products—the sort of accumulation induced by the fetishistic consumption inherent in the capitalist system, by the dominant ideology, and by advertising and having nothing to do with some "eternal human nature."

As capitalism, especially in its current neoliberal and globalized form, seeks to commodify the world, to transform everything existing—earth, water, air, living creatures, the human body, human relationships, love, religion—into commodities, so advertising aims to sell those commodities by forcing living individuals to serve the commercial necessities of capital. Both capitalism as a whole and advertising as a key mechanism of its rule involve the fetishization of consumption, the reduction of all values to cash, the unlimited accumulation of goods and of capital, and the mercantile culture of the "consumer society." The sorts of rationality involved in the advertising system and the capitalist system are intimately linked, and both are intrinsically perverse.

Advertising pollutes the mental landscape, just like it does the urban and rural landscapes; it stuffs the skull like it stuffs the mailbox. It holds sway over press, cinema, television, radio. Nothing escapes its decomposing influence: in our time we see that sports, religion, culture, journalism, literature, and politics are ruled by advertising. All are pervaded by advertising's attitude, its style, its methods, its mode of argument. Meanwhile, we are always and uninterruptedly harassed by advertising: without stop, without truce, unrelentingly and never taking a vacation, advertising persecutes us, pursues us, attacks us in city and countryside, in the street and at home, from morning to evening, from Monday to Sunday, from January to December, from the cradle to the grave.

Yet this advertising is nothing but a tool, an instrument of capital used to dispose of its output, to unload its shoddy goods, to make its investments pay, to expand its profit margins, and to win "sectors of the market." Advertising does not exist in a vacuum: it is an essential part, a crucial gear in the capitalist system of production and consumption. Without capitalism, advertising would have no reason to exist: it could not persist into a postcapitalist society for even an instant. Inversely, capitalism without advertising would be like a machine with sand in its gears.

Let us add, in passing, that while advertising did not exist in the countries whose bureaucratically planned economies vanished after the Berlin Wall fell, there was a mendacious political propaganda that was no less inhuman and repressive. That too must be avoided in any transition to a postcapitalist society.

Still, today's omnipresent commercial advertising is inextricably intertwined with capitalism. It is capitalist corporations that design, finance, and profit from advertising campaigns and that "sponsor"— that is to say, pollute via advertising—newspapers, television, athletic competitions, and cultural events. Advertising plays the role of tub-thumper, pimp, and zealous servant for the interests of capital: "Our aim," explained the chief executive of TF1 (the leading French commercial TV channel), "is to be selling Coca-Cola during all the time our viewers' brains are at our disposal."[25] Capitalism and advertising, inseparably intertwined, are the authors and active promoters of the commodification of the world, of the commercialization of social relations, of the monetization of the soul.

What, then, is advertising's impact on the environment? The French ecological NGO Alliance pour la Planète (Alliance for the Planet) is rightly upset by advertising's use of fraudulent "environmentalist" arguments to greenwash everything: nuclear power stations, genetically modified organisms, automobiles, and soon—why not?—road haulage. For opponents of advertising, this is not exactly news: we have long known that advertising lies as naturally as it breathes. Not because of deficient morality among those gentlemen advertisers, but because of the intrinsically perverse nature of the advertising system. Mystification and manipulation of consciousness are, alas, the sole justification for its existence: advertising that does not lie is an animal as hard to find as a vegetarian crocodile. As to the Bureau de Verification de la Publicité (the Bureau for Truthfulness in Advertising) in France, consisting entirely of representatives from advertising corporations, its credibility and effectiveness are about on par with a Bureau for Safe Henhouses consisting entirely of worthy delegates from the Brotherhood of Foxes. Nevertheless, phony green advertising is but the tip of the iceberg. It is for more fundamental, structural reasons that the advertising machine is a dangerous enemy of the environment. Here are two such reasons:

1. Advertising is an immense, fearsome waste of our planet's limited resources. In France alone, advertising expenditures amount to several tens of billions of euros, more than the state budgets of many African countries. With such a sum, it would be possible to build thousands of child-care centers, hospitals, schools, and homes, to begin solving the unemployment problem, to give large-scale aid to the Third World. How many millions of acres of forest are cut down in the world every year to print the ever-increasing mass of advertising brochures cluttering our mailboxes or to make billboards and posters covering the walls of our streets and hiding our countryside? How many hundreds of millions of kilowatt-hours are expended each year by the neon advertisements "embellishing" our cities, from Shanghai to New York (not forgetting Paris)? How many tons of garbage left behind by this activity? How many millions of tons of greenhouse gases emitted to supply the energy needs of the advertising circus? And so on. The damages, though hard to calculate, are undoubtedly gigantic. And what purpose does this enormous waste serve? To convince the public that detergent X washes whiter than detergent Y. Does this make sense? Of course not, but it's profitable (for advertisers). If you're looking for a sector of the economy that is useless, that could easily be eliminated without any harm to the populace while saving

great outlays on energy and raw materials—what better example than the advertising industry? Certainly, that would involve laying off very many people but, rather than condemning them to unemployment, they could usefully be hired for new "green" jobs.

2.   All environmentalists agree in denouncing the "consumerism" of the Western (i.e., advanced capitalist) countries as one of the main causes of the ecological disaster threatening us. But they don't know how to alter that state of things: By making buyers feel guilty? By preaching frugality? By willingly making one's own life an example of austerity? All are legitimate activities, but they have a very limited impact on the larger public and even run the risk, in certain cases, of making people less willing to comply with environmental requirements. A change in consumption habits will not be accomplished in a day: it is a social process that will take years. It cannot be imposed from on high, nor can it be left merely to the virtuous "good will" of private individuals. It involves a true political battle in which active education by the public authorities must play a role. But the main agents of change will be education and struggles by consumer associations, trade unions, environmental movements, and—why not?—political parties. One of the crucial fronts in this battle is the fight for a complete and definitive suppression of advertising imperialism, that gigantic undertaking to colonize our minds and our behaviors, whose terrible effectiveness cannot be overestimated.

As we have seen, advertising is one of the main factors responsible for the obsessive consumption of modern societies, of the ever more irrational tendency toward piling up (usually useless) material goods—in short, of a perfectly unsustainable consumption paradigm. Compulsive consumption is one of the essential driving forces for the process of expansion and unlimited "growth" that have always characterized modern capitalism and now are driving us, with ever-increasing speed, toward the abyss of global warming. It is thus not by chance that the publishers of one of the most inventive "adverphobic" magazines in recent years, *Adbusters*, have also started the environmentalist magazine *Objecteurs de Croissance* (*Conscientious Objectors to Growth*): advertising harassment and unlimited growth are two inseparable dimensions of the system, two teats from which capital accumulation feeds. It follows that transformation of the current consumption paradigm is closely linked to struggle against the tentacles of advertising. How can people be convinced to abandon consumption habits incompatible with ecological equilibrium without putting a stop to the continuous pounding of advertising that incites, encourages, and stimulates them night and day to buy and buy again? How can individuals shake off the culture of conspicuous consumption—famously studied at the turn of the century by the American economist Thorstein Veblen—that tells them they can affirm their personalities only by buying and displaying supposedly "exclusive" products, except by freeing them from the advertising that incessantly reproduces this reified culture? How can the public be freed from the dictatorship of "fashion" that forces the speedy obsolescence of products, themselves ever more ephemeral, without taking on the head-stuffing—if not brainwashing—of advertising? How can we put an end to the tyranny of brands, the neurotic obsession with logos, without breaking up advertising's frightful Ubuesque "brainectomy" machine?

The compulsive consumerist behavior in advanced capitalist society is not the manifestation of "human nature" or of some innate tendency of individuals to consume more and ever more. Nothing comparable is ever found in precapitalist communities or societies; it is specific to capitalist modernity and inseparable from the dominant fetishistic ideology, from the religious cult of commodity worship actively promoted by the advertising system. What that manufactures is not merely the desire to acquire this or that product—it is a culture, a worldview, habits, behaviors. In short, a whole way of life.

Rather than seeking to force individuals to "lower their standard of living" or "reduce their consumption"—an abstract, merely quantitative approach—what is needed is to create conditions under which people can, little by little, discover their real needs and qualitatively change their ways of consumption: for example, by choosing more culture, education, health, or home improvement rather than buying new gadgets, new decreasingly useful commodities. For this, the suppression of harassment by advertising is a necessary condition.

Of course, this is still not sufficient. For example, consider the iconic commodity of so-called Fordist capitalism, the private automobile, whose harmfulness to the general environment—by air pollution, paving over green spaces, and above all forcing climate change through carbon dioxide emissions—needs no demonstration. Steady reduction of its place in our cities—to be democratically decided by the public itself—can successfully be brought about only if, in parallel with the suppression of the persistent and mendacious advertising for automobiles, urban planning strongly favors alternative means of transport: mass transit, bicycles, pedestrianism.

Advertising is an essential gearing in the infernal neoliberal/capitalist spiral of ever-increasing, ever-expanding (*Expansion* is the title of a prestigious corporate business magazine) production/consumption/accumulation—that spiral that is driving the exponentially increasing degradation of the environment—degradation that leads us, by means of climate change, to a catastrophe without precedent in human history. Advertising can even be viewed as the oil lubricating those terribly efficacious gears that are crushing the planet and might well, in a few decades, render it uninhabitable for humans.

The moral of the story is this: a different world is possible, beyond capitalist reification, commodity fetishism, and advertising. But we cannot wait for it to arrive: the struggle for a different future begins here and now. Every attempt to put limits to advertising's aggression—until we are able, one day, to get rid of it altogether—is an environmental duty, a political and moral imperative for all those who hope to save our natural environment from destruction. The fight for a different civilizational paradigm is to be waged precisely through that sort of initiative. We fight, henceforth, to rein back advertising's frenzy, in the same way that anticapitalists mobilize for measures—the Tobin Tax, for example—that would apply the brakes to the unlimited covetousness of capital. Each success, even if limited, if won through collective action, is a step in the right direction and, above all, an advance in the people's acquisition of consciousness and self-organization—the main condition for total transcendence of the system.

CHAPTER FOUR

Chico Mendes and the Brazilian Struggle for the Amazonian Forest

The Amazonian rainforest is a decisive component of the earth's ecological equilibrium; it has not only the largest existing compound of biodiversity, but also a key factor in the absorption of carbon dioxide, slowing down the process of climate change. The resistance of Indigenous and peasant communities against its destruction has, therefore, a vital importance for humanity as a whole.

During the last years of the military dictatorship in Brazil a protest movement began to appear, first among small peasants living from the extraction of natural products, against the local or multinational capitalist forces of agribusiness interested in destroying the rainforest: cattle ranchers, soybean planters, wood merchants, and all sort of *latifundistas* (big landowners) who wanted to uproot or burn the trees and expel the people.

Chico Mendes was the leader of this resistance. He has since become a legendary figure, a hero of the Brazilian people. However, the mainstream narratives of his story tend to hide the radical character of his struggle or to ignore its double dimension: social-liberal ecologists forget his socialist commitment, while the productivist left leaves out the ecological one.

Born on December 15, 1944, in the town of Xapuri, in the Brazilian state of Amazonas, Francisco Alves Mendes Filho—his full name—was educated at first by the Christian liberationist culture of the Brazilian Comunidades Eclesiais de Base (CEBs), or basic ecclesial communities. During the 1960s he would discover Marxism, with the help of an old Communist fighter, Euclides Fernandes Tavora, a former lieutenant who had followed Luís Carlos Prestes to take part in the "Red" armed uprising of 1935—an action for which he paid with years in prison and, later, exile in Bolivia. After clandestinely returning to Brazil, Tavora lived near the Bolivian border, in the Amazonian region. This Marxist apprenticeship had a decisive influence on the formation of Mendes's political ideas: according to his own words, meeting Tavora "was a very great help and one of the reasons why I take part in this struggle. Not all comrades had, at that time, the privilege to receive such an important orientation for their future as I did."

Chico Mendes worked as a *seringueiro*, one of the small-scale rubber-tappers who lived by collecting latex from Amazonian rubber trees. In 1975 he founded, together with Wilson Pinheiro, the Brasiléia Rural Workers' Union and, soon afterward in 1977, the

Xapuri Rural Workers' Union, in the town where he was born. During those years that he began using, along with his union comrades, a form of nonviolent struggle without precedent elsewhere: the famous *empates* (standstills). Hundreds of seringueiros, with their wives and children, would hold hands and confront, without weapons, the bulldozers of the big companies interested in deforestation. Sometimes the rubber-tappers were defeated, but often they were able to stop, with their naked hands, the Caterpillars, bulldozers, and electric saws of the forest-killers, sometimes even winning the support of the laborers in charge of the deforestation. The enemies of the seringueiros and other people of the forest are the latifundistas, agribusiness, the wood-exporting companies, and the cattle ranchers—who also raise beef for export—who want to bring down the trees in order to sell the wood and/or replace the forest with pastures for cattle. The political branch of this powerful enemy is the so-called Democratic Rural Union (UDR) and its armed branch, the mercenary *jagunços* (hired gunmen), and there is collusion within the police, the justice system, and the governments (local, regional, and federal). During those years Chico Mendes received his first death threats; soon enough, in 1980, his comrade in struggle Wilson Pinheiro was murdered.

During the first years of his union activity, Mendes, a convinced socialist, joined the Communist Party of Brazil, which was a Maoist split from the old Brazilian Communist Party. He was soon disappointed with this party, which he said preferred, at the moment of struggle and confrontation with the landowners, "to hide behind the curtains." In 1979 he joined the new Workers' Party (PT), founded by Luiz Inácio Lula da Silva (known as Lula, a future president of Brazil) and his comrades, where Mendes belonged to the left wing.

In 1982 he ran for Parliament as the local PT candidate but was not elected, the party being, at that time, still in its beginnings.

In 1985, with the end of the dictatorship, the rubber-tappers were able to organize a National Council of Seringueiros, which received the support of the Catholic Pastoral Land Commission, the PT, and the newly formed Landless Workers' Movement (Movimento dos Trabalhadores Rurais Sem Terra, or MST). To build a larger force, Mendes took the initiative to unite the seringueiros and other workers who lived from the forest by extracting nuts and other products with the Indigenous communities and various peasant groups, founding the Forest Peoples Alliance. For the first time, rubber-tappers and Indigenous people, who had fought each other so many times in the past, united their forces against the common enemy. Chico Mendes defined the foundations of this Alliance: "Never again will one of our comrades spill the blood of the others; together we can protect nature, the forest, which is where we all learned to live, to raise our children, and to develop our capacities in harmony with nature, with the environment, and with all beings which live here."[26]

A pragmatic man of action, an organizer and fighter, concerned with practical and concrete issues—launching literacy campaigns, founding cooperatives, searching for viable economic alternatives—Chico was also a dreamer and a utopian, in the noble and revolutionary sense of the word. It is impossible to read without emotion his socialist and internationalist testament, devoted to future generations and published soon after his death by the Xapuri union:

> Attention, young people of the future: September 6 of the year 2120, anniversary of the first centennial of the world socialist revolution, which unified all the peoples of the planet around one

ideal and one thought of socialist unity, and which put an end to all enemies of the new society. Here remains only the remembrance of a sad past of pain, suffering, and death. Forgive me. I was only dreaming when I described these events, which I won't be able to see. But I had the pleasure of having a dream.[27]

The Alliance proposed a sort of agrarian reform adapted to the conditions of the Amazonian rainforest, with both ecological and socialist characteristics: the land would become public property, while the peasants and Indigenous communities would have the free use of it (usufruct).

Chico Mendes was perfectly conscious of the ecological dimension of this struggle, which interested not only the peoples of the Amazon but the entire world population, which depends on the tropical forest—the green "lungs" of the planet. As he wrote in his autobiography, "We discovered that in order to assure the future of the Amazon forest, one had to create a reserve where only small-scale extraction would be permitted. . . . We, the seringueiros, understand that it is urgent to stop the deforestation that threatens the Amazon and therefore the life of all the peoples in the planet."[28]

In 1987, some US ecological organizations invited Chico Mendes to come speak as a witness before a meeting of the Inter-American Development Bank. In the name of his Alliance he denounced the projects the international banks financed, which were destroying sections of the Amazonian rainforest. From this moment on, he became widely known and that year he received the United Nations Environmental Program Global 500 Roll of Honor Award. The struggle of the Forest Peoples Alliance became a symbol of the planetary mobilization to save the last great rainforest of the world.

In 1988 the National Conference of the CUT, the Brazilian Workers' Trade Union Confederation, approved a thesis Mendes presented in the name of the National Council of Seringueiros under the title *Defense of Nature and of the Forest Peoples*. Its main demand was both ecological and social:

> the immediate expropriation of the *seringais* (latex plantations) in conflict, which should be given to the peasant communities who live from the extraction; this way nature and the culture of the rainforest peoples will not be aggressed and a sustainable use of the natural resources will be possible, thanks to technologies developed centuries ago by the people who live from the extraction of natural products from the Amazonian forest.[29]

The Forest Peoples Alliance obtained at this time two important victories: establishing the first protected rainforest areas reserved for small-scale extraction activities (*reservas extrativistas*) in the state of Acre, and expropriating a seringal at Cachoeira, near Xapuri, belonging to the latifundista Darly Alves da Silva.

Chico Mendes considered this to be a significant achievement of the movement:

> The most important thing to stimulate the continuity of this movement was the victory of the rubber-tappers of Cachoeira. This victory had a positive impact on the whole region, because the rubber-tappers knew they were fighting against the most powerful enemy and his gangs of bloodthirsty killers. They knew that they were struggling against a death squad, and even so they were not afraid. Some days we had as many as 400 rubber-tappers assembled in a picket line in the middle of the forest.[30]

For the rural oligarchy, which for centuries had been used to "getting rid" of "troublemakers" (that is, those who dare to organize the rural laborers to fight against the latifundium) with complete impunity, this was unbearable. In December 1988 Chico Mendes was assassinated by a killer paid by the Alves da Silva landowners.

After the murder of Chico Mendes, the Forest Peoples Alliance continued, with ups and downs, and is still present several decades later. Even though it was not able to stop the disastrous process of destruction on a general scale, its combination of socialism and ecology, agrarian reform and defense of the Amazonian forest, peasant and Indigenous struggles, the survival of humble local populations and the protection of a heritage of humanity—the last great tropical forest not yet destroyed by capitalist "progress"—made Chico Mendes's movement an example that will continue to inspire new struggles, not only in Brazil but in many other countries and continents. Chico Mendes's most amazing feat is that he very quickly became aware of the ecological dimension of his struggle and succeeded, with others, in shaping a convergence between ecological arguments and landownership demands. The Forest Peoples Alliance soon found itself at the forefront of promoting alternative models of development, symbolized by models of socio-environmentalism that combine sustainable management of natural resources with the valorization of local practices and knowledge.

CHAPTER FIVE

Ecosocial Struggles of Indigenous Peoples

Indigenous communities have become the center of the struggle for the environment in Latin America. This is true not only because of their local actions in defense of rivers and forests against petroleum and mining multinationals, but also because they propose an alternative way of life to that of neoliberal globalized capitalism. Indigenous peoples in particular may be the ones undertaking these struggles, but they quite often do so in alliance with landless peasants, ecologists, socialists, and Christian communities, with support from unions, left parties, the Pastoral Land Commission, and the Indigenous Pastoral Ministry.

The dynamics of capital require the transformation of all commonly held goods into commodities, which sooner or later leads to destruction of the environment. The petroleum zones of Latin

America, abandoned by the multinationals after years of exploitation, are poisoned and destroyed, leaving behind a dismal legacy of illnesses among the inhabitants. It is thus completely understandable that the populations living in the most direct contact with the environment are the first victims of this ecocide and are attempting to oppose the destructive expansion of capital, sometimes successfully.

Indigenous peoples' resistance, then, has very concrete and immediate motivations—to save forests or water resources—in their battle for survival. However, it also corresponds to a deep antagonism between the cultures, ways of life, spirituality, and values of these communities and the "spirit of capitalism" as Max Weber defined it: the subjection of all activity to profit calculations, profitability as the sole criterion, and the quantification and reification (*Versachlichung*) of all social relations. There is a sort of "negative affinity" between Indigenous ethics and the spirit of capitalism—the converse of the elective affinity between the Protestant ethic and capitalism, a profound sociocultural opposition. Certainly, there are Indigenous or *Métis* communities that adapt to the system and try to gain from it. Furthermore, Indigenous struggles involve extremely complex processes, including identity recomposition, transcoding of discourses, and political instrumentalization, all of which deserve to be closely studied. Yet we can clearly see that a continuous series of conflicts characterizes the relations between Indigenous populations and modern capitalist agricultural or mining corporations. This conflict has a long history. It is admirably described in a novel by the anarchist writer B. Traven, *The White Rose*, which narrates how a large North American oil company seized the lands of a Mexican Indigenous community after murdering its leader.[31] However, the conflict has intensified during the last few decades because of both the intensity and the extent of capital's exploitation of the environment, and also because of the rise of the global justice movement—which took on this struggle—and the Indigenous movements of the continent.

World Social Forum of Belém in the Brazilian Amazon (2009)

Twenty years after Chico Mendes's murder, the struggle to defend the Amazon forest spread and was organized around the entire global justice movement. Indigenous Latin American movements have often participated in global justice initiatives and in the World Social Forums (WSFs) held in Porto Alegre. A key moment, however, was the WSF held in Belém in the state of Pará—the second-largest city of the Brazilian Amazon, with more than one million inhabitants—in January 2009. For the first time, and as the WSF organizers intended, there was a huge and sudden emergence of Indigenous communities and traditional populations in the global justice movement. Their demands and their diagnosis of the "crisis of Western capitalist civilization" were at the center of all Forum debates. The WSF adopted their slogan in the face of the increasing pace of destruction of the Amazon forest by wood exporters, large landowners raising livestock, and soy and petroleum corporations: "Zero Deforestation Now!"

A general assembly of Indigenous delegates approved an important document, the "Declaration of Indigenous Peoples at the World Social Forum: Appeal from the Indigenous Peoples Facing the Capitalist Crisis of Western Civilization." This appeal was signed by dozens of peasant, Indigenous, and global justice organizations, mainly from the Americas, at the suggestion of Andean organizations from Peru, Ecuador, and Bolivia, countries where the majority of the population is of Amerindian origin. This document breaks with dominant "progressive" responses, which seek to validate and reinforce the role of the state and are based on plans for economic revival. Its aim is to fight against the commodification of life by defending "Mother Earth" and the struggle for collective rights, "living well," and decolonization—all responses to the crisis of Western capitalist civilization.

During the Social Forum, an international ecosocialist declaration concerning climate change signed by hundreds of people from several countries was distributed to the participants. Following the close of the WSF, an Ecosocialist Conference was held in Belém on February 2, 2009, with the participation of a large delegation of Indigenous people from Peru. It was coordinated by Hugo Blanco, historic leader of peasant and Indigenous struggles in Peru and former member of the Peruvian Constituent Assembly, and Marcos Arana, a priest linked with liberation theology and Indigenous movements—honored in 2004 with the Peruvian National Human Rights Award and suspended by the Church hierarchy because of his sociopolitical commitments. In his presentation, Hugo Blanco recalled that Indigenous communities have fought for several centuries for the same objectives as ecosocialism: specifically, collective agricultural organization and respect for Mother Earth.

The increasingly important place of Indigenous populations and their territories within international organizations, from the local to the global levels, is expressed above all in local struggles that are quite symbolic of the originality of ecological and political processes in Latin America.

Examples of Local Struggles: Peru, 2008–12

There are an impressive number of conflicts listed on the website of the Observatory of Latin American Mining Conflicts (Observatorio de Conflictos Mineros de América Latina, or OCMAL). These conflicts pit Indigenous and peasant communities from Mexico to Tierra del Fuego against various petroleum or mining companies, mainly North American or European multinationals. Two examples from Peru illustrate the dynamics of these types of confrontations. Peru is, like Bolivia and Ecuador, a Latin American country where the majority of the population is of Indigenous origin. However, unlike the other two Andean countries, Indigenous movements have never succeeded in inspiring true political change and forcing recognition of their sociocultural demands. Yet these movements have continued to lead persistent struggles over many years against the multinationals responsible for environmental destruction and the governments that support them. Two recent examples illustrate these conflicts. In June 2008, a confrontation between the government and Indigenous people took place in Bagua, Peru. The communities rose up against the decree of Alan García's neoliberal government that applied Peru's free-trade agreement with the United States to authorize petroleum and wood-exporting corporations to exploit the forests of the Andes and the Amazon. The García government fiercely cracked down on the protest by the Interethnic Association for the Development of the Peruvian Rainforest (La Asociación Interétnica de Desarrollo de la Selva Peruana, or AIDESEP, the main organization of Amazon Indigenous communities), which led to many deaths.

In 2011, a change in government occurred with the election of the nationalist candidate Ollanta Humala, who promised to break with his predecessor's neoliberal policies and submission to multinational interests. He inherited from his predecessor the Conga Project, which allows the mining corporation Yanacocha—owned by the North American multinational Newmont, known for its disturbing past of pollution and contempt for human rights in different countries, in partnership with local companies—to exploit an open-air gold mine. The predictable result of the Conga Project is pollution—or rather poisoning—of rivers, directly threatening the survival of local communities. Little by little, concerned communities mobilized against the project, developing around the slogan "Yes to water, no to gold!" Indigenous and peasant women were at the forefront, organizing demonstrations of tens of thousands of participants behind banners that said "No to Conga!" Indigenous leaders like Blanco and Arana showed solidarity with this struggle and tried to give it international recognition. Faced with protests from the Indigenous communities, which were supported by civil society, Humala's government chose to respond harshly in 2012 with military repression, killing several demonstrators, imprisoning the mayor of Cajamarca for having supported the local communities, and even (more recently) having Marcos Arana publicly beaten by armed police. Protests took place all over Latin America and also in Europe. OCMAL denounced the assassination of demonstrators and the imprisonment of two human-rights lawyers. This affair illustrates the "neo-extractionist"—and repressive—logic of Peruvian governments of various political persuasions and the stubborn resistance of Indigenous populations.[32]

The Yasuní National Park Project: Ecuador, 2007–13

One of the most important actions by Indigenous movements and ecologists in Latin America is the Yasuní National Park Project in Ecuador. The park is huge: 9,280 square kilometers of virgin forest. Extraordinarily rich in terms of biodiversity—botanists have calculated that one hectare of this forest contains more species of trees than the entire United States—it is inhabited by Indigenous communities and delimited by three small cities: Ishpingo, Tambococha, and Tiputini (hence the abbreviation ITT to designate the whole area). After drilling in the Yasuní region, various petroleum companies, notably including the Maxus Energy Corporation of Texas, found three large petroleum reserves with an estimated capacity of 850 million barrels. Previous Ecuadoran governments had, in the 1980s and 1990s, granted concessions to the Texaco, but the resistance of Indigenous communities had limited the damage by preventing most of the drilling.

The proposal of the Indigenous movement was to leave the petroleum in the ground, thereby avoiding 400 million tons of carbon dioxide emissions, in exchange for compensation from the international community. Concretely, the wealthy countries would be responsible for half of the expected receipts, around $3.5 billion over thirteen years. The money would be paid to a fund managed by the United

Nations Development Programme (UNDP) and exclusively earmarked for preserving biodiversity and developing renewable energies. Indigenous and ecological movements initially put this project forward, but it was only after Rafael Correa's election in 2007 that it was to be implemented under the initiative of Alberto Acosta, then minister of mines. The Yasuní project was one of the only initiatives at the international level that actually responded to the urgency of the fight against climate change by offering a measure that is, at the very least, effective: to leave the petroleum in the ground. This measure is much more efficient than the "market for emission allowances" and other "clean development mechanisms" in the Kyoto accords, which have proved to be completely incapable of significantly reducing greenhouse gases.[33] In the case of Yasuní Park—as in most Indigenous struggles, particularly in the Amazon region—local communities' fight to defend their environment from the destructive voraciousness of the fossil-fuel oligarchy has coincided completely with the great ecological cause of the twenty-first century: preventing global warming, one of the greatest threats ever known to human life on the planet.

Countries from the North, which are supposed to be taking measures to restrict emissions of greenhouse gases, were not much interested in Ecuador's heterodox proposal. A few European countries—Spain, Italy, and Germany—paid a total of three million dollars: a long way to go! Further, some countries—notably Italy and Norway—have canceled $100 million of Ecuador's external debt.[34] Faced with these lukewarm results, Rafael Correa decided in September 2013 to give up the project and open the park to oil corporations. However, large mobilizations by Indigenous peoples, peasants, and ecologists, supported by the left, protested the decision and are calling for a referendum on the issue.

If the wealthy countries have shown such little enthusiasm for the project, it is not only because the project has nothing to do with their preferential "market mechanisms" but also, above all, because they fear the demonstration effect of this initiative. Agreeing to finance Yasuní would be tantamount to opening the door to hundreds of similar projects—projects in complete contradiction with the policies advanced capitalist countries have chosen. This is illustrated quite well by the (non-) choices they have made in the various climate conferences, where the inability of the countries of the North to change direction is obvious. This inability, moreover, has prompted a notable reaction by South American peoples, concretized in the organization of the World People's Conference on Climate Change in Cochabamba in 2010.

World People's Conference on Climate Change: Cochabamba, Bolivia, 2010

During the United Nations Climate Change Conference in Copenhagen (2009), Evo Morales, the Indigenous president of Bolivia, was the only head of government to support the demonstrations occurring in the streets of the Danish capital under the slogan "Change the system, not the climate!"

In response to the failure of the Copenhagen conference, a World People's Conference on Climate Change and the Rights of Mother Earth was convened at Morales's initiative in the Bolivian city of Cochabamba in April 2010. At the beginning of the 2000s, this city had been the site of victorious struggles against water privatization (the "Water War"). More than twenty thousand delegates participated from all over the world, though the majority came from the Andean countries of Latin America, with a very substantial Indigenous representation. The resolution the conference adopted, which has had considerable international effect, expresses the ecological and anticapitalist ideas of Indigenous movements, even in the terminology it uses. Here are some extracts from this document:

> The capitalist system has imposed on us a logic of competition, progress and limitless growth. This regime of production and consumption seeks profit without limits, separating human beings from nature and imposing a logic of domination upon nature, transforming everything into commodities: water, earth, the human genome, ancestral cultures, biodiversity, justice, ethics, the rights of peoples, and life itself.
>
> Under capitalism, Mother Earth is converted into a source of raw materials, and human beings into consumers and a means of production, into people that are seen as valuable only for what they own, and not for what they are.
>
> Capitalism requires a powerful military industry for its processes of accumulation and imposition of control over territories and natural resources, suppressing the resistance of the peoples. It is an imperialist system of colonization of the planet.
>
> Humanity confronts a great dilemma: to continue on the path of capitalism, depredation, and death, or to choose the path of harmony with nature and respect for life.
>
> It is imperative that we forge a new system that restores harmony with nature and among human beings. And in order for there to be balance with nature, there must first be equity among human beings.
>
> We propose to the peoples of the world the recovery, revalorization, and strengthening of the knowledge, wisdom, and ancestral practices of Indigenous Peoples, which are affirmed in the

thought and practices of "Living Well," recognizing Mother Earth as a living being with which we have an indivisible, interdependent, complementary and spiritual relationship.[35]

One can criticize the mystical and confused aspect of the concept of "Mother Earth" (*Pachamama* in the Indigenous languages Aymara and Quechua), as some leftist Latin American intellectuals have done, or point out the impossibility of giving an effective legal expression to the "rights of Mother Earth," as jurists have done. Yet this would be to lose sight of the essential point: the powerful, radically anti-systemic social dynamic that has crystallized around these slogans.

Among the terms that have appeared in Indigenous discourse over the past few years, the one that seems to have the widest acceptance is *kawsay sumak* or *buen vivir* (living well). This is a *qualitative* conception of the "good life" based on the satisfaction of real social needs and respect for nature as opposed to the capitalist cult of growth, expansion, and "development," accompanied by the consumer obsession of "always more." The concepts of the "rights of Mother Earth" and *buen vivir* rapidly spread not only to Indigenous and ecological currents, but also to the entire global justice movement. Eventually, they were included in the constitutions of Bolivia and Ecuador by the progressive governments of these two countries.

These examples of Indigenous peoples' struggles, summit meetings, and alternative proposals seem to be promising paths toward a post-petroleum transition and alternative models of development that are lacking more than ever in this period of systemic crisis. However, these advances should not be allowed to hide the contradictions of these movements and, above all, of these governments.

The Contradictions of South American Leftist Governments

Many Latin American countries have left or center-left governments; most—Brazil, Uruguay, Nicaragua, El Salvador, Chile, etc.—do not go beyond the limits of *social-liberalism*, a policy that remains within the limits of neoliberal orthodoxy, favoring the interests of banks, multinationals, and agribusiness but at the same time implementing some redistribution of the rent for the benefit of the most disadvantaged strata. Ecology is not at all a priority for these governments. Their main objective remains capitalist: "growth" and "development."

The Brazilian government, first under the leadership of Luiz Inácio Lula da Silva, "Lula," the head of the Workers' Party, and now under President Dilma Rousseff of the same party, is a good example of these policies. Marina Silva—a friend of Chico Mendes—resigned in 2008 as Lula's environmental minister, citing her inability to obtain even a minimum of guarantees for protection of the Amazon forest. Favoring agribusiness—the large capitalist producers of soybeans, cattle, and sugarcane for export—instead of the peasant agriculture, Lula and Dilma have permitted the expansion of environmentally destructive practices on a large scale.

One symbol of the Brazilian government's harmful choices for the environment and Indigenous populations is the construction of the Belo Monte Dam, which will be the third-largest dam complex in the world. Construction is under way despite thirty years of fierce and extremely well-organized struggles by the traditional populations who live in the Xingu River basin.[36] Brazil is also embarking on a dangerous and gigantic project of extracting oil from large reserves found several miles under the sea; there has never been an attempt to drill oil in such a deep site, under the salt level of the seabed. This can easily lead to massive oil spills, much worse than the recent ones in the Gulf of Mexico. Since the area is uninhabited, it is much more difficult to mobilize against this project, which will substantially increase Brazil's contribution to global warming. Brazilian unions and social movements protested the concession of drilling rights to multinational corporations, but only a handful of ecosocialists challenged the project itself.

Some countries, however, like Venezuela, Bolivia, and Ecuador, have attempted to break with neoliberal policies and have confronted the interests of the oligarchy and multinationals. All these anti-imperialist and anti-oligarchic governments recognize the importance of ecological challenges and are disposed to take measures to safeguard the environment. However, all three of their governmental budgets remain totally dependent on returns from fossil fuels (gas and petroleum), the fuels responsible for climate change. The Venezuelan government has hardly examined this issue; the absence of a sizeable or organized Indigenous population at the sites of exploitation is one of the reasons for this lack. Certainly, by prohibiting industrial fishing—which destroys all marine fauna—to the benefit of small-scale fishing, the Chavez government took an important ecological measure. However, the exploitation of petroleum, which includes all its "dirtiest" forms, continues without interruption, and there are few efforts to develop alternative energies.

In the two Andean countries, Bolivia and Ecuador, debate around the alternatives of "neo-extractionism or environment" lies at the heart of social and political confrontations. In Bolivia, Evo Morales's commitment to the struggle against climate change and in defense of Mother Earth does not always correspond with the concrete practices of the Bolivian government, which is attached to a development strategy in which gas production and mining activities occupy an important place. Recently, a project to construct a highway that would cross a large area of virgin forest provoked energetic protests from local Indigenous communities, leading to the (temporary) suspension of the project. Vice President Álvaro García Linera, who in his youth spent years in jail for fighting in the Indigenous Tupak Katari guerilla movement, branded the protesting communities enemies of progress and national development, manipulated by NGOs at the service of foreign interests.

The Ecuadorian example shows how easily such progressive governments can sacrifice the environment in the interest of oil profits. By abandoning the Yasuní project and opening the forest for the multinational fossil-fuel oligarchy, Rafael Correa illustrates the limitations of these governments from the viewpoint of a coherent ecosocial agenda, their tendency to favor short-range gains, and their submission to the imperative of "growth" at any price.

It is reasonable for ecosocialists and anticapitalists to support these governments, whatever their limits and contradictions, against their right-wing, oligarchic, and pro-imperialist enemies, but this can only be critical support, considering how far these experiences are from an effective socialist and ecological perspective. Surely, it would be unrealistic to ask the governments of Venezuela, Bolivia, and Ecuador to immediately stop oil (or gas) production, since this is, at the moment, the main source for financing their significant social programs. But they could take some partial initiatives concerning specific areas, such as the Yasuní Park project, in order to set a positive example for other parts of the world on how to fight climate change by leaving the fossil energies under the soil and putting pressure on the rich countries of the North, with the demand of indemnities for the unexploited oil.

These, alongside other socioecological measures—scrapping GMOs, agrotoxics, water-polluting mines, forest devastation, and so on—will take place only if there is sufficient pressure from autonomous social movements and public opinion on the leftist governments. Indigenous communities can play a decisive role here if they are able to keep their autonomy, refuse to subordinate themselves to the governments, however progressive and anti-imperialist, and supersede a purely local perspective to develop a broad, systemic, anticapitalist, ecosocial agenda. The Cochabamba conference of 2010, despite its limits, shows that this is possible. Building large coalitions with peasant movements, labor unions, youth networks, ecologists, feminists, ecosocialists, and others is also key to Indigenous communities' efficacy. Of course, there is no guarantee that they will succeed, but they represent the hope of an alternative road for Latin America.

Conclusion

Indigenous communities are at the forefront of efforts to defend virgin forests, rivers, and the general environment against powerful adversaries: fossil-fuel multinationals, mining corporations, and agribusiness companies. In addition, the cultures, ways of life, and languages of Indigenous peoples have marked the discourse and culture of social and ecological movements, Social Forums, and global justice networks in Latin America. Finally, governments that claim to be leftist in countries with large Indigenous populations have taken on, to a certain extent, Indigenous ecological discourse, yet they continue to practice an "extractionist" model of development.

APPENDIX 1

International Ecosocialist Manifesto

The twenty-first century opens on a catastrophic note, with an unprecedented degree of ecological breakdown and a chaotic world order beset with terror and clusters of low-grade, disintegrative warfare that spread like gangrene across great swathes of the planet—viz., central Africa, the Middle East, northwestern South America—and reverberate throughout the nations. In our view, the crises of ecology and those of societal breakdown are profoundly interrelated and should be seen as different manifestations of the same structural forces.

The former broadly stems from rampant industrialization that overwhelms the earth's capacity to buffer and contain ecological destabilization. The latter stems from the form of imperialism known as globalization, with its disintegrative effects on societies that stand in its path. Moreover, these underlying forces are essentially different aspects of the same drive, which must be identified as the central dynamic that moves the whole: the expansion of the world capitalist system.

By Joel Kovel and Michael Löwy (September 2001)

We reject all euphemisms or propagandistic softening of the brutality of this regime: all greenwashing of its ecological costs, all mystification of the human costs under the names of democracy and human rights.

We insist instead upon looking at capital from the standpoint of what it has really done.

Acting on nature and its ecological balance, the regime, with its imperative to constantly expand profitability, exposes ecosystems to destabilizing pollutants, fragments habitats that have evolved over eons to allow the flourishing of organisms, squanders resources, and reduces the sensuous vitality of nature to the cold exchangeability required for the accumulation of capital.

From the side of humanity, with its requirements for self-determination, community, and a meaningful existence, capital reduces the majority of the world's people to a mere reservoir of labor power while discarding much of the remainder as useless nuisances.

It has invaded and undermined the integrity of communities through its global mass culture of consumerism and depoliticization.

It has expanded disparities in wealth and power to levels unprecedented in human history.

It has worked hand in glove with a network of corrupt and subservient client states whose local elites carry out the work of repression while sparing the center of its opprobrium.

And it has set going a network of transtatal organizations under the overall supervision of the Western powers and the superpower United States, to undermine the autonomy of the periphery and bind it into indebtedness while maintaining a huge military apparatus to enforce compliance to the capitalist center.

We believe that the present capitalist system cannot regulate, much less overcome, the crises it has set going. It cannot solve the ecological crisis because to do so requires setting limits upon accumulation—an unacceptable option for a system predicated upon the rule: Grow or Die!

And it cannot solve the crisis posed by terror and other forms of violent rebellion because to do so would mean abandoning the logic of empire, which would impose unacceptable limits on growth and the whole "way of life" sustained by empire. Its only remaining option is to resort to brutal force, thereby increasing alienation and sowing the seed of further terrorism . . . and further counterterrorism, evolving into a new and malignant variation of fascism.

In sum, the capitalist world system is historically bankrupt. It has become an empire unable to adapt, whose very gigantism exposes its underlying weakness. It is, in the language of ecology, profoundly unsustainable, and must be changed fundamentally, nay, replaced, if there is to be a future worth living.

Thus the stark choice once posed by Rosa Luxemburg returns: Socialism or Barbarism!, where the face of the latter now reflects the imprint of the intervening century and assumes the countenance of ecocatastrophe, terror, counterterror, and their fascist degeneration.

But why socialism, why revive this word seemingly consigned to the rubbish heap of history by the failings of its twentieth-century interpretations?

For this reason only: that however beaten down and unrealized, the notion of socialism still stands for the supersession of capital. If capital is to be overcome, a task now given the urgency of the survival of civilization itself, the outcome will perforce be "socialist," for that is the term which signifies the breakthrough into a postcapitalist society.

If we say that capital is radically unsustainable and breaks down into the barbarism outlined above, then we are also saying that we need to build a "socialism" capable of overcoming the crises capital has set going. And if socialisms past have failed to do so, then it is our obligation, if we choose against submitting to a barbarous end, to struggle for one that succeeds.

And just as barbarism has changed in a manner reflective of the century since Luxemburg enunciated her fateful alternative, so too must the name, and the reality, of a socialism become adequate for this time.

It is for these reasons that we choose to name our interpretation of socialism as an ecosocialism, and dedicate ourselves to its realization.

Why Ecosocialism?

We see ecosocialism not as the denial but as the realization of the "first-epoch" socialisms of the twentieth century, in the context of the ecological crisis. Like them, it builds on the insight that capital is objectified past labor, and grounds itself in the free development of all producers, or to use another way of saying this, an undoing of the separation of the producers from the means of production.

We understand that this goal was not able to be implemented by first-epoch socialism, for reasons too complex to take up here, except to summarize as various effects of underdevelopment in the context of hostility by existing capitalist powers. This conjuncture had numerous deleterious effects on existing socialisms, chiefly, the denial of internal democracy along with an emulation of capitalist productivism, and led eventually to the collapse of these societies and the ruin of their natural environments.

Ecosocialism retains the emancipatory goals of first-epoch socialism, and rejects both the attenuated, reformist aims of social democracy and the productivist structures of the bureaucratic variations of socialism. It insists, rather, upon redefining both the path and the goal of socialist production in an ecological framework.

It does so specifically in respect to the "limits on growth" essential for the sustainability of society. These are embraced not, however, in the sense of imposing scarcity, hardship, and repression. The goal, rather, is a transformation of needs and a profound shift toward the qualitative dimension and away from the quantitative. From the standpoint of commodity production, this translates into a valorization of use values over exchange values—a project of far-reaching significance grounded in immediate economic activity.

The generalization of ecological production under socialist conditions can provide the ground for the overcoming of the present crises. A society of freely associated producers does not stop at its own democratization. It must, rather, insist on the freeing of all beings as its ground and goal. It overcomes thereby the imperialist impulse both subjectively and objectively.

In realizing such a goal, it struggles to overcome all forms of domination, including, especially, those of gender and race. And it surpasses the conditions leading to fundamentalist distortions and their terrorist manifestations. In sum, a world society is posited in a degree of ecological harmony with nature unthinkable under present conditions.

A practical outcome of these tendencies would be expressed, for example, in a withering away of the dependency upon fossil fuels integral to industrial capitalism. And this in turn can provide the material point of release of the lands subjugated by oil imperialism, while enabling the containment of global warming, along with other afflictions of the ecological crisis.

No one can read these prescriptions without thinking, first, of how many practical and theoretical questions they raise, and second and more dishearteningly, of how remote they are from the present configuration of the world, both as this is anchored in institutions and as it is registered in consciousness.

We need not elaborate these points, which should be instantly recognizable to all. But we would insist that they be taken in their proper perspective.

Our project is neither to lay out every step of this way nor to yield to the adversary because of the preponderance of power it holds. It is, rather, to develop the logic of a sufficient and necessary transformation of the current order, and to begin developing the intermediate steps toward this goal.

We do so in order to think more deeply into these possibilities and, at the same moment, begin the work of drawing together with all those of like mind. If there is any merit in these arguments, then it must be the case that similar thoughts, and practices to realize these thoughts, will be coordinatively germinating at innumerable points around the world.

Ecosocialism will be international and universal, or it will be nothing. The crises of our time can and must be seen as revolutionary opportunities, which it is our obligation to affirm and bring into existence.

The Belém Declaration

The following declaration was prepared by a committee elected for this purpose at the Paris Ecosocialist Conference of 2007 consisting of Ian Angus, Joel Kovel, Michael Löwy, with the help of Danielle Follett. It was distributed at the World Social Forum in Belém, Brazil, in January 2009.

The declaration was supported by more than four hundred activists from thirty-four countries. Their signatures are at the bottom of this appendix.

We encourage supporters to distribute the Declaration widely, and to translate it into their languages. It is currently available online in

- French
- Greek
- Italian
- Portuguese
- Turkish

The Belém Declaration

"The world is suffering from a fever due to climate change, and the disease is the capitalist development model."
—Evo Morales, president of Bolivia, September 2007

Humanity's Choice

Humanity today faces a stark choice: ecosocialism or barbarism.

We need no more proof of the barbarity of capitalism, the parasitical system that exploits humanity and nature alike. Its sole motor is the imperative toward profit and thus the need for constant growth. It wastefully creates unnecessary products, squandering the environment's limited resources and returning to it only toxins and pollutants. Under capitalism, the only measure of success is how much more is sold every day, every week, every year—involving the creation of vast quantities of products that are directly harmful to both humans and nature, commodities that cannot be produced without spreading disease, destroying the forests that produce the oxygen we breathe, demolishing ecosystems, and treating our water, air, and soil like sewers for the disposal of industrial waste.

Capitalism's need for growth exists on every level, from the individual enterprise to the system as a whole. The insatiable hunger of corporations is facilitated by imperialist expansion in search of ever greater access to natural resources, cheap labor, and new markets. Capitalism has always been ecologically destructive, but in our lifetimes these assaults on the earth have accelerated. Quantitative change is giving way to qualitative transformation, bringing the world to a tipping point, to the edge of disaster. A growing body of scientific research has identified many ways in which small temperature increases could trigger irreversible, runaway effects—such as rapid melting of the Greenland ice sheet or the release of methane buried in permafrost and beneath the ocean—that would make catastrophic climate change inevitable.

Left unchecked, global warming will have devastating effects on human, animal, and plant life. Crop yields will drop drastically, leading to famine on a broad scale. Hundreds of millions of people will be displaced by droughts in some areas and by rising ocean levels in others. Chaotic, unpredictable weather will become the norm. Air, water, and soil will be poisoned. Epidemics of malaria, cholera, and even deadlier diseases will hit the poorest and most vulnerable members of every society.

The impact of the ecological crisis is felt most severely by those whose lives have already been ravaged by imperialism in Asia, Africa, and Latin America, and indigenous peoples everywhere are especially vulnerable. Environmental destruction and climate change constitute an act of aggression by the rich against the poor.

Ecological devastation, resulting from the insatiable need to increase profits, is not an accidental feature of capitalism: it is built into the system's DNA and cannot be reformed away. Profit-oriented production only considers a short-term horizon in its investment decisions, and cannot take into account the long-term health and stability of the environment. Infinite economic expansion is incompatible with finite and fragile ecosystems, but the capitalist economic system cannot tolerate limits on growth; its constant need to expand will subvert any limits that might be imposed in the name of "sustainable development." Thus the inherently unstable capitalist system cannot regulate its own activity, much less overcome the crises caused by its chaotic and parasitical growth, because to do so would require setting limits upon accumulation—an unacceptable option for a system predicated upon the rule: Grow or Die!

If capitalism remains the dominant social order, the best we can expect is unbearable climate conditions, an intensification of social crises, and the spread of the most barbaric forms of class rule, as the imperialist powers fight among themselves and with the global South for continued control of the world's diminishing resources.

At worst, human life may not survive.

Capitalist Strategies for Change

There is no lack of proposed strategies for contending with ecological ruin, including the crisis of global warming looming as a result of the reckless increase of atmospheric carbon dioxide. The great majority of these strategies share one common feature: they are devised by and on behalf of the dominant global system, capitalism.

It is no surprise that the dominant global system which is responsible for the ecological crisis also sets the terms of the debate about this crisis, for capital commands the means of production of knowledge, as much as that of atmospheric carbon dioxide. Accordingly, its politicians, bureaucrats, economists, and professors send forth an endless stream of proposals, all variations on the theme that the world's ecological damage can be repaired without disruption of market mechanisms and of the system of accumulation that commands the world economy.

But a person cannot serve two masters—the integrity of the earth and the profitability of capitalism. One must be abandoned, and history leaves little question about the allegiances of the vast majority of policy-makers. There is every reason, therefore, to radically doubt the capacity of established measures to check the slide to ecological catastrophe.

And indeed, beyond a cosmetic veneer, the reforms over the past thirty-five years have been a monstrous failure. Isolated improvements do of course occur, but they are inevitably overwhelmed and swept away by the ruthless expansion of the system and the chaotic character of its production.

One example demonstrates the failure: in the first four years of the twenty-first century, global carbon emissions were nearly three times as great per annum as those of the decade of the 1990s, despite the appearance of the Kyoto Protocols in 1997.

Kyoto employs two devices: the "cap and trade" system of trading pollution credits to achieve certain reductions in emissions, and projects in the global South—the so-called "clean development mechanisms"— to offset emissions in the highly industrialized nations. These instruments all rely upon market mechanisms, which means, first of all, that atmospheric carbon dioxide becomes a commodity under the control of the same interests that created global warming. Polluters are not compelled to reduce their carbon emissions, but allowed to use their power over money to control the carbon market for their own ends, which include the devastating exploration for yet more carbon-based fuels. Nor is there a limit to the amount of emission credits which can be issued by compliant governments.

Since verification and evaluation of results are impossible, the Kyoto regime is not only incapable of controlling emissions, it also provides ample opportunities for evasion and fraud of all kinds. As even the *Wall Street Journal* put it in March 2007, emissions trading "would make money for some very large corporations, but don't believe for a minute that this charade would do much about global warming."

The Bali climate meetings in 2007 opened the way for even greater abuses in the period ahead. Bali avoided any mention of the goals for drastic carbon reduction put forth by the best climate science (90 percent by 2050); it abandoned the peoples of the global South to the mercy of capital by giving jurisdiction over the process to the World Bank; and made offsetting of carbon pollution even easier.

In order to affirm and sustain our human future, a revolutionary transformation is needed, where all particular struggles take part in a greater struggle against capital itself. This larger struggle cannot remain merely negative and anticapitalist. It must announce and build a different kind of society, and this is ecosocialism.

The Ecosocialist Alternative

The ecosocialist movement aims to stop and to reverse the disastrous process of global warming in particular and of capitalist ecocide in general, and to construct a radical and practical alternative to the capitalist system. Ecosocialism is grounded in a transformed economy founded on the nonmonetary values of social justice and ecological balance. It criticizes both capitalist "market ecology" and productivist socialism, which ignored the earth's equilibrium and limits. It redefines the path and goal of socialism within an ecological and democratic framework.

Ecosocialism involves a revolutionary social transformation, which will imply the limitation of growth and the transformation of needs by a profound shift away from quantitative and toward qualitative economic criteria, an emphasis on use value instead of exchange value.

These aims require both democratic decision making in the economic sphere, enabling society to collectively define its goals of investment and production, and the collectivization of the means of production. Only collective decision making and ownership of production can offer the longer-term perspective that is necessary for the balance and sustainability of our social and natural systems.

The rejection of productivism and the shift away from quantitative and toward qualitative economic criteria involve rethinking the nature and goals of production and economic activity in general. Essential creative, nonproductive, and reproductive human activities, such as householding, child-rearing, care, child and adult education, and the arts, will be key values in an ecosocialist economy.

Clean air and water and fertile soil, as well as universal access to chemical-free food and renewable, nonpolluting energy sources, are basic human and natural rights defended by ecosocialism. Far from being "despotic," collective policy-making on the local, regional, national, and international levels amounts to society's exercise of communal freedom and responsibility. This freedom of decision constitutes a liberation from the alienating economic "laws" of the growth-oriented capitalist system.

To avoid global warming and other dangers threatening human and ecological survival, entire sectors of industry and agriculture must be suppressed, reduced, or restructured and others must be developed, while providing full employment for all. Such a radical transformation is impossible without collective control of the means of production and democratic planning of production and exchange. Democratic decisions on investment and technological development must replace control by capitalist enterprises, investors, and banks, in order to serve the long-term horizon of society's and nature's common good.

The most oppressed elements of human society, the poor and indigenous peoples, must take full part in the ecosocialist revolution, in order to revitalize ecologically sustainable traditions and give voice to those whom the capitalist system cannot hear. Because the peoples of the global South and the poor in general are the first victims of capitalist destruction, their struggles and demands will help define the contours of the ecologically and economically sustainable society in creation. Similarly, gender equality is integral to ecosocialism, and women's movements have been among the most active and vocal opponents of capitalist oppression. Other potential agents of ecosocialist revolutionary change exist in all societies.

Such a process cannot begin without a revolutionary transformation of social and political structures based on the active support, by the majority of the population, of an ecosocialist program. The struggle of labor—workers, farmers, the landless, and the unemployed—for social justice is inseparable from the struggle for environmental justice. Capitalism, socially and ecologically exploitative and polluting, is the enemy of nature and of labor alike.

Ecosocialism proposes radical transformations in:

1. the energy system, by replacing carbon-based fuels and biofuels with clean sources of power under community control: wind, geothermal, wave, and, above all, solar power;

2. the transportation system, by drastically reducing the use of private trucks and cars, replacing them with free and efficient public transportation;

3. present patterns of production, consumption, and building, which are based on waste, inbuilt obsolescence, competition, and pollution, by producing only sustainable and recyclable goods and developing green architecture;

4. food production and distribution, by defending local food sovereignty as far as this is possible, eliminating polluting industrial agribusinesses, creating sustainable agro-ecosystems, and working actively to renew soil fertility.

To theorize and to work toward realizing the goal of green socialism does not mean that we should not also fight for concrete and urgent reforms right now. Without any illusions about "clean capitalism," we must work to impose on the powers that be—governments, corporations, international institutions—some elementary but essential immediate changes:

- drastic and enforceable reduction in the emission of greenhouse gases,
- development of clean energy sources,
- provision of an extensive free public transportation system,
- progressive replacement of trucks by trains,
- creation of pollution clean-up programs, and
- elimination of nuclear energy and war spending.

These and similar demands are at the heart of the agenda of the global justice movement and the World Social Forums, which have promoted, since Seattle in 1999, the convergence of social and environmental movements in a common struggle against the capitalist system.

Environmental devastation will not be stopped in conference rooms and treaty negotiations: only mass action can make a difference. Urban and rural workers, peoples of the global South, and indigenous peoples everywhere are at the forefront of this struggle against environmental and social injustice, fighting exploitative and polluting multinationals, poisonous and disenfranchising agribusinesses, invasive genetically modified seeds, biofuels that only aggravate the current food crisis. We must further these social-environmental movements and build solidarity between anticapitalist ecological mobilizations in the North and the South.

This Ecosocialist Declaration is a call to action. The entrenched ruling classes are powerful, yet the capitalist system reveals itself every day more financially and ideologically bankrupt, unable to overcome the economic, ecological, social, food, and other crises it engenders. And the forces of radical opposition are alive and vital. On all levels, local, regional, and international, we are fighting to create an alternative system based in social and ecological justice.

◆ ◆ ◆

We, the undersigned, endorse the analysis and political perspectives outlined in the Belém Ecosocialist Declaration, and support the establishment and building of an Ecosocialist International Network.

◆ ◆ ◆

Aotearoa/New Zealand: Don Archer, Bronwen Beechey, Grant Brookes, Joe Carolan, Roger Fowler, Vaughan Gunson, Bernie Hornfeck, Peter Hughes, Greg Kleis, Daphne Lawless, James McDonald, Grant Morgan, Len Parker, Paul Piesse, Tony Snelling-Berg

Australia: Richard Bergin, Jamie Brown, Simon Butler, Ben Courtice, Felicity Crombach, Peter Cummins, John B. Ellis, Duroyan Fertl, Jepke Goudsmit, Stu Harrison, Dave Kimble, Serge Leroyer, Günter Minnerup, John Rice, Larissa Roberts, Stuart Rosewarne, Terry Townsend

Bangladesh: A. F. Mujtahid, Mohammad Basir-ul Haq Sinha

Belgium: Daniel Tanuro

Brazil: Eduardo d'Albergaria, Carlos Henrique Rodrigues Alves, Berlano Bênis França de Andrade, João Claudio Arroyo, Pedro Ivo de Souza Batista, Luiz Felipe Bergmann, Lucas Bevilaqua, Leonel da Costa Carvalho, Francisco Marcos Bezerra Cunha, Ricardo Framil Filho, Giuliana Iarrocheski, Iolanda Toshie Ide, Edson Carneiro Indio, Beatriz Leandro, Ivonaldo Leite, André Lima, Isabel Loureiro, Jorge Oliveira, Ricardo Oliveira, Marcos Barbosa de Oliveira, Maicon Fernando Palagano, Paulo Piramba, Fabio Mascaro Querido, Valdir Pereira Ribeiro Júnior, Carmen Sylvia Ribeiro, Fatima Terezinha Alvarenga Rivas, Marechal Cândido Rondon, Roberto Souza Santos, Dhyana Nagy Teodoro, Thierry Thomas, Carolina Kors Tiberio, Julio Yamamoto

Canada, Quebec: Greg Albo, Robert Albritton, Paul Anderson, Ian Angus, Roger Annis, Chris Arsenault, Charles-Antoine Bachand, Jean-Claude Balu, Rick Barsky, José Bazin, John R. Bell, Shannon Bell, John L. Bencze, Karl Beveridge, Geoff Bickerton, Leigh Brownhill, David Camfield, William K. Carroll, John Clarke, Bill Clennett, Carole Condé, Phil Cournoyer, Paul R. Craik, Steve D'Arcy,

Susan Kent Davidson, Diane Delaney, Kathleen Donovan, Kevin Doyle, Joseph Dubonnet, Susan E. Ferren, Richard Fidler, Blair Fix, Darrel Furlotte, Larry Gambone, Cy Gonick, Trevor Goodger-Hill, Joyce A. Green, Dave Greenfield, Ricardo Grinspun, John Grogan, Dr. J. Robert Groves, Adam Hanieh, Trevor Harrison, Henry Heller, Evert Hoogers, Pete Huerter, Catherine Hughes, Anton Oscar Iorga, Sean Isaacs, Darlene Juschka, Michael A. Lebowitz, Ian B. McKenna, Cindy Morrison, Vincent Mosco, Dan Murray, Sam Noumoff, Derrick O'Keefe, Joseph Roberts, Sheila Roberts, Leo Panitch, Tomislav Peric, Ursula Pflug, Roger Rashi, John Riddell, Rowland Keshena Robinson, Herman Rosenfeld, Rhoda Rosenfeld, Laina Rutledge, John Ryan, Kanchan Sarker, Bob Sass, Scott Schneider, Sid Shniad, Debra Scott, John Sharkey, John Shavluk, Dr. Christopher A. Shaw, Michael Stewart, Debra Tacium, Paul Francis Thompson, David Tremblay, Terisa E. Turner, Jesse Vorst, Bernadette L. Wagner, Len Wallace, John W. Warnock, Larry Watt, Barry Weisleder, Ian Whyte, Sarah Wilbur, Michael Wolfe, Paul York

Chile: Benjamin Leiva

Cyprus: Julian Saurin

Denmark: Pelle Andersen-Harild, Ellen Brun, Jacques Hersh, Peder Hvelplund, Kjeld A. Larsen, Leif Leszczynski, Johannes Lund, Karolina Boroch Naess, Petter Naess, Teresa Naess, Carsten Pedersen

El Salvador: Ricardo Adan Molina Meza

England, Scotland, Wales: Tobias Abse, Keith Ames-Rook, Keith Baker, Oscar Blanco Berglund, Simon Boxley, Jane Burd, Katie Buse, Dr. Michael Calderbank, Ross Carbutt, James Doran, Ian Drummond, Jane Susanna Ennis, Dan Fredenburgh, Ed Fredenburgh, Nick Foster, Paul Frost, Colin Fox, Giorgos Galanis, Jay Ginn, Dr. Joseph Healy, Dave Hewitt, Stuart Jeffery, Jane Kelly, Aaron Kiely,

Richard Kuper, David McBain, Jade McClune, Sharon McMaster, Tony Medwell, Shosh Morris, Elaine Morrison, Jamie Murray, Brian Orr, Andy Player, Julian Prior, Matt Sellwood, Mike Shaughnessy, Andrew Stevens, Sally Thompson, Sean Thompson, Alan Thornett, Payam Torabi, Norman Traub, Mike Tucker, Derek Wall, Roy Wilkes

Finland: Marko Ulvila

France: Jean-Frédéric Baeta, Michel Benquet, Thierry Bonhomme, Richard Bouillet, Noelle Calvinhac, Nadège Edwards, Carole Engel, Hendrik Davi, Cedric Dulski, Armand Farrachi, Danielle Follett, Vincent Gay, Laurent Garrouste, Jacques Giraldou, Jacques Giron, Xavier Granjon, Richard Greeman, Bernard Guibert, Michel Husson, Raoul-Marc Jennar, Fahima Laidondi, Marianne Ligou, Michael Löwy, Marilou Mertens, Roxanne Mitrallias, Jean-Philippe Morin, Arno Münster, Jacques Muriel, Carsten Rank, André Rosevegue, Pierre Rousset, Michael Le Sauce, Peter Shield, Mohammed Taleb, Hugo Valls

Germany (Deutschland): Ruth Birkle, Sebastian Gerhardt, Werner Hager, Angela Klein, Peter Schüren, Dr. Michael Rieger, Frieder Otto Wolf

Greece (Hellas): Mesrop Abelyan, Vasilis Andronis, Makis Choren, Spyros Diamantidis, Anneta Galtsioti, Krystalia Galtsioti, Giannis Galtsiotis, Konstantina Georga, Dimitris Georgas, Kostas Giannakakis, Hasan Mehedi, Manolis Kapadais, Andonis Krinis, Amjad Mohammad, Georgia Nikopolidou, Takis Pantazidis, Tasos Pantazidis, Eleni Pantazidou, Katerina Pantazidou, Mohammed Es Sabiani, Stefanos Sinaplidis

Haiti: Maxime Roumer

India: Debashis Chatterjee, Debal Deb, S. Susan Deborah, Sushovan Dhar, Mita Dutta, Merlin Franco, Saroj Giri, C. E.

Karunakaran, Partha Majumdar, D. V. Natarajan, V. T. Padmanab-
han , Bijay Panda, Sukla Sen, Babu Lal Sharma

Indonesia: Yanuarius Koli Bau, Pius Ginting

Ireland: Louis P. Burns a.k.a. Lugh, Domhnall Ó Cobhthaigh,
Vincent Doherty

Italy: Guido Dalla Casa, Moreno Esposto

Kenya: Arege Douglas

Malta: Michael Briguglio

Mexico: David Barkin, Gerardo Renique

Netherlands: Willem Bos, Suzanne de Kuyper, Peter Waterman

Panama: Sebastián Calderón Bentin, Antonio Salamaca Serrano

Peru: Hugo Blanco

Portugal: Ana Bastos, Rita Calvário, Ricardo Coelho, Ronaldo
Fonseca, José Carlos Alves Loureiro, Ângelo Novo, Pedro Ramajal

Romania: Luisa Abram, Stella Dicu, Mario Festila

Serbia: Dragoslav Danilovic

South Africa: Rasigan Maharajh, Karthie Mudaly, Trevor Ng-
wane, Berend Schuitema

Spain: Mauricio Blechman, Francisco Fernández Amador, Alberto Iglesias Lorenz

Switzerland: Juan Tortosa

Turkey: Ertugrul Akcaoglu, Nevra Akdemir, Levent Gürsel Alev,
Binnur Aloglu, Rana Aribas, Ecehan Balta, Emre Baturay Altinok,
Ugur Arigun, Arca Atay, Baris Avci, Erol Bayrakdar, Foti Benlisoy,
Stefo Benlisoy, Elif Bozkurt, Emel Budak, Ozgur Bulut, Çaglayan
Büyükçula, Nurgül Çanak, Esin Candan, Bilge Contepe, Gülsüm
Coskun, Kadir Dadan, Fügen Dede, Evin Deniz, Yalim Dilek, Sinan
Eden, Huseyin Eren, Fuat Ercan, Basak Ergüder, Bulent Erkeskin,
Firat Genç, Emine Girgin, Canan Güldal, Ercan Gülen, Ibrahim

Gundogdu, Kutlay Gürcihan, Muharrem Hunerli, Taha Karaman, Filiz Kerestecioglu, Olcay Halk Kiliç, Tarkan Kilic, Ekoloji Kolektifi, Sinem Meral, Özgür Müftüoglu, Evin Nas, Sebnem Oguz, Pinar Ongan, Kazim Özaslan, Merthan Özcan, Recep Özkan, Ali Murat Ozdemir, Gökçen Özdemir, Senem Pehlivanoglu, Inci Polat, Özge Savas, Hasan Sen, Ahmet Hamdi Seringen, Yavuz Selim Sertbas, Eren Deniz Tol-Gokturk, Dr. Ethem Torunoglu, Eylem Tuncaelli, Kemal Tuncaelli, Feriha Tugran, Mehmet Türkay, Derya Ülker, Tanay Sidki Uyar, Sanem Yardimci, Ertan Yilmaz, Gaye Yilmaz, Selim Yilmaz, Burçak Yilmazok, Hatice Yaşar, Kasim Yeter, Eylem Ozen Yorukoglu, Semih Yuksel, Kizilca Yurur

Uruguay: Alejandro Casas

USA: Anatole Anton, Matthew Brown, Joaquín Bustelo, Tim Casebolt, Suha Chari, Andrew P. Cheramie, Tom Collins, Stan Cox, Kevin Danaher, Dr. Lenore J. Daniels, Jennifer Dignazio, Daniel Faber, Hunter Gray [Hunter Bear], Craig Brozefsky, John Clark, Scott Davis, W. Alexander Durnan, Stefan Furrer, Phil Gasper, Dayne Goodwin, Sarah Grey, Anthony Gronowicz, Timoteo Jeffries, Eric W. Koch, Bill Koehnlein, Joel Kovel, Ed Laing, Larry Lambert, Saul Landau, James Lauderdale, Mark A. Lause, Richard Levins, Kevin Lewis, Timothy Norbert Malczynski, David Marcial, Michael Seth Martin, Stefan Mattessich, Bill McCormick, Coleman E. Mc-Farland, Fred Mecklenburg, William Meurer, Curtis Moore, Jonathan Nack, Simeon Newman, Tony Nizzi, Ivan Olsen, Julia O'Neal, Wren Osborn, Dr. Marie-Claire Picher, Louis Proyect, Linda Ray, Idrian N. Resnick, Kat Rickenbacker, Christine J. Rodgers, Eugene Rodriguez, Christian Roselund, Kevin Ruffe, David Schwartzman, Javier Sethness, Barry Sheppard, Roger Sheppard, Laurence H. Shoup, Rick Sklader, Skip Slavik, James Smith,

Mark E. Smith, Red Son, Anna Marie Stenberg, Carl Stilwell, Ted Stolze, Michael Tanzer, Idell Elaine Vogel, Richard Vogel, Sam Waite, Ron Warren

Venezuela: Elías Capriles, Gustavo Fernández Colón, Carlos García, Dalia Correa Guía, Miguel Angel Contreras Natera, Jesus Pirela, Cesar Aponte Rivero,Isabel Villarte

Zimbabwe: Chen Chimutengwende

APPENDIX 3

Copenhagen 2049

This document was prepared, thanks to H.G. Wells' time machine, by the Ecosocialist International Network, www.ecosocialistnetwork.org. The draft was written by Michael Löwy, with the help of Klaus Engert, Danièle Follet, Joel Kovel, Joaquín Nieto and Ariel Salten.

COPENHAGEN, APRIL 12, 2049

Illustrated by Sille Stenersen Hansen

April 12, 2049. It was a nice, cool spring morning, temperature did not rise above 41.2 C in the shadow. Grandmother Sarah, aged 71, went for a walk on the sea-shore with her grandson Stefan, aged 10. They engaged in a very lovely conversation.

Stefan: Grandmother, is it true what father told me this morning, that under the sea in front of all of us is a whole city which was once called Copenhagen?

Sarah: Yes, dear Stefan. It was a charming town full of palaces, churches, towers, theatres, universities. We used to live there with our friends and family before the Catastrophe.

Stefan: What happened?

Sarah: Did you not learn about it in school? The greenhouse gases resulting from the fossil energies — coal, oil — produced a rise in temperature, and the billions of tons of ice from the South Pole and Greenland melted. It started slowly, but some years ago it became a sudden process. Enormous blocks of ice slipped into the sea and the Ocean's level rose by several meters.

Stefan: I see - Did it only happen here in Denmark?

Sarah: Oh no, my child. It happened all around the world. Many other wonderful towns like Vienna, Amsterdam, London, New York, Rio de Janeiro, Buenos Aires, Hong-Kong are now under the sea...

Stefan: Will I never see Copenhagen and these other beautiful cities?

Sarah: I'm afraid not, Stefan. Some scholars say that in a few thousand years, when the climate will change again, the sea may retrocede, revealing the ruins of those splendid towns. But we won't be there to see.

Stefan: Our grandmother, did nobody foresee the Catastrophe?

Sarah: Many people did! 40 years ago some scientists like James Hansen, the climatologist of the NASA, pretty accurately predicted what would happen, if we would continue with "business as usual." Other scientists also predicted what had happened in Southern Europe: instead of the green lands of South Italy, France and Spain, we now have the so-called Southern European Sahara Desert.

Stefan: Tell me grandmother, was the Catastrophe inevitable?

Sarah: Not really, sonny. Some decades ago it was still possible to avert it, if radical changes had been done.

Stefan: Why didn't the governments take some initiatives at the time?

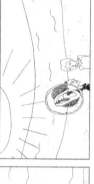

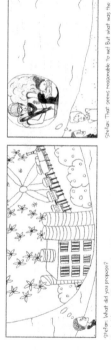

Sarah: Most of them served the interests of the ruling classes who refused to consider any change that threatened their economic system — the capitalist market economy — their privileges and their way of life. They were a sort of "fossil oligarchy". They clung desperately to oil and coal and considered any proposal of quickly replacing them by renewable alternatives such as solar energy, as "unrealistic" or as a threat to the "competitiveness" of their enterprises. They decided to establish a poor "Emissions rights trading system, where big polluters bought the right to continue polluting.

Stefan: How could they be so blind?

Sarah: Look, in 2009 when the town of Copenhagen still existed, the rulers of the world met here for a World Conference on Climate Change. They made beautiful speeches, but did not come to any significant conclusions on what to do the next few years. Some rich industrial countries announced that by 2050 they would reduce their emissions of green-house gases by half! Meanwhile, they decided to establish a poor "Emissions rights trading system, where big polluters bought the right to continue polluting.

Stefan: And nobody protested?

Sarah: Of course, there were protests! Masses of angry people came from all of Europe, and also from far away countries. To Copenhagen. They voiced their protest and called for immediate and radical measures, such as a reduction of emissions by 40% till 2020. We should have asked for 80%! Among the people supporting these measures there were some — I was one of them! — who called themselves ecosocialists.

Stefan: What did you propose?

Sarah: We argued that a radical social change was needed, taking the means of production from the hands of the capitalist oligarchy to give them to the people. We called for a new mode of civilisation, a new pattern of production — using solar energy — and of consumption, suppressing advertisement and the useless junk it promoted. Instead of unlimited "growth", based on unlimited profit and accumulation of capital, we proposed the democratic planning of production, according to the real social needs, and the protection of the environment!

Stefan: That seems reasonable to me! But what was the response of the authorities?

Sarah: Well, we and all the young protesters were received with police clubs and tear gas.

Stefan: Did you get hit, grandmother?

Sarah: Oh yes! I was hit by a cop with a rubber truncheon, and my left ear was almost cut. Look, I still have a mark here, under my hair.

The Lima Ecosocialist Declaration

Declaration of the Ecosocialist International Network before COP20, to be held in Lima, Peru, December 2014

Our lives are worth more than their profits!

The imminent climate crisis that we confront today is a grave threat to the preservation of life on the planet. Many academic and political works have confirmed the fragility of life on earth to temperature change. Only a few degrees can cause—and are causing—an ecological catastrophe of incalculable consequences. Now we are experiencing the deadly effects of this situation. The melting ice, the contamination of the atmosphere, rising sea levels, desertification,

---

Translated by Quincy Saul for Ecosocialist Horizons, affiliate of the Ecosocialist International Network.

and the increasing intensity of the weather, are all proof.

It is now fundamental to ask ourselves who and what is causing the climate to change like this. We urgently need to unmask all the abstract answers, which attempt to blame all of humanity. These abstract answers disconnect the current situation from the historical dynamics which have emerged from fossil fuel (coal, oil, gas)–based industrialization, which causes global warming, and the logic of capitalism, which is sustained by the private appropriation of wealth and the conquest of profit. Profit at the cost of social exploitation and ecological devastation: these are two faces of the same system, which is the culprit of climate catastrophe.

In this panorama, the Conference of the Parties (COP), organized by diverse governments and funded by large corporations, confirms the responsibility of capitalism for the climate crisis by putting on empty events without any effective resolutions capable of solving the problem. In fact, we are moving backwards, a retreat expressed in the ridiculous "green funds" which openly profit from pollution. Sadly, this dynamic is deepened through the attitudes sustained by multiple governments—facilitating pollution and putting the profits of corporations above the wellbeing of people. This can be seen most strongly in the countries of the South, and thus it is fundamental to comprehend that the dynamics of this system tend to dump the global ecological crisis upon the shoulders of the oppressed and exploited of the earth.

It is vital to emphasize the importance of the diverse social and ecological struggles all over the world, which propose to stop climate change and the ecological crisis through the logic of solidarity. It is important to note that many of these processes are launched and led by women. Without a doubt, the Latin American scenario today exemplifies the mix of resistance, self-management, and processes of transformation, based on projects which can unite new proposals with ancestral cosmovisions. One example can be found in the brave struggles of the indigenous peoples and *campesinos* of Peru, in particular their resistance to the Conga mega-mining project. It is also useful to focus our attention on the experience of the Yasuní Park, which was the initiative of Indigenous and ecological movements—to protect a large region of Amazon rainforest from oil drilling, in exchange for payments from rich nations to the people of Ecuador. The government of Rafael Correa accepted the proposal for several years, but recently decided to open the park to multinational oil corporations, provoking important protests. Another case can be found in the development projects which the Brazilian government is attempting to carry out, which threaten a large part of Amazonia with destruction.

From this perspective, there is very little to hope for at COP20 this December in Lima, Peru. If there is any escape from climate change and the global ecological crisis, it will emerge from the power of struggle and the organization of the oppressed and exploited peoples of the world, with the understanding that the struggle for a world without ecological devastation must connect to the struggle for a society without oppression or exploitation. This change must begin now, bringing together unique struggles, daily efforts, processes of self-management, and reforms to slow the crisis, with a vision centered on a change of civilization, a new society in harmony with nature. This is the central proposal of ecosocialism, an alternative to our current ecological catastrophe.

Change the system, not the climate!

◆ ◆ ◆

Signatures:

Argentina: Manuel Ludueña, Paulo Bergel

Belgium: Christine Vanden Daelen, Daniel Tanuro

Brazil: Joao Alfredo de Telles Melo, Marcos Barbosa, José Corrêa, Isabel Loureiro, Renato Roseno, Renato Cinco, Henrique Vieira, Flávio Serafini, Alexandre Araújo, Carlos Bittencourt, Renato Gomes

Canada: Jonatas Durand Folco (Quebec), Terisa Turner

Spain: Esther Vivas (Cataluña), Jaime Pastor, Justa Montero, Mariano Alfonso, Teresa Rodrigues, Manuel Gari, Jorge Riechmann, Joaquin Vega

United States: Ariel Salleh, *Capitalism Nature Socialism*, Joel Kovel, Leigh Brownhill, Quincy Saul, Salvatore Engel Di Mauro, Terran Giacomini

France: Christine Poupin, Dominique Cellier, Henrik Davi, Mathieu Agostini, Michel Bello, Michael Löwy, Vincent Gay, Laurent Garrouste, Sophie Ozanne

Greece: Yorgos Mitralias, Panos Totsikas

Mexico: Andrés Lund, Samuel González Contreras, José Efraín Cruz Marín

Norway: Anders Ekeland

Peru: Hugo Blanco

País Vasco (Basque Country): Iñigo Antepara, Josu Egireun, Mikel Casado, Sindicato ELA, Ainhara Plazaola

Switzerland: Juan Tortosa, Mirko Locatelli, Anna Spillmann, Félix Dalang

Notes

1. Editorial, "Let Them Eat Pollution," *Economist* (February 8, 1992).
2. Richard Smith, "The Engine of Eco Collapse," *Capitalism Nature Socialism* 16(4) (2005): 35.
3. Karl Marx, *Das Kapital*, vol. 1 (Berlin: Dietz Verlag, 1960), 529–30. For a remarkable analysis of the destructive logic of capital, see Joel Kovel, *The Enemy of Nature: The End of Capitalism or the End of the World?* (New York: Zed Books, 2002).
4. James O'Connor, *Natural Causes: Essays in Ecological Marxism* (New York: Guilford Press, 1998), 278, 331.
5. John Bellamy Foster uses the concept of "ecological revolution," but he argues that "a global ecological revolution worthy of the name can only occur as part of a larger social—and I would insist, socialist—revolution. Such a revolution . . . would demand, as Marx insisted, that the associated producers rationally regulate the human metabolic relation with nature. . . . It must take its inspiration from William Morris, one of the most original and ecological followers of Karl Marx, from Gandhi, and from other radical, revolutionary and materialist figures, including Marx himself, stretching as far back as Epicurus." Foster, "Organizing Ecological Revolution," *Monthly Review*, 57(5) (2005): 9–10.
6. For an ecosocialist critique of "actually existing ecopolitics"—green economics, deep ecology, bioregionalism, etc.—see Joel Kovel, *The*

Enemy of Nature, 2nd ed. (London: Zed Books, 2007), chapter 7.

7.   See John Bellamy Foster, *Marx's Ecology: Materialism and Nature* (New York: Monthly Review Press, 2000).

8.   Friedrich Engels, *Anti-Dühring* (Paris: Ed. Sociales, 1950), 318.

9.   Marx, *Das Kapital*, vol. 3 (Berlin: Dietz Verlag, 1968), 828, and vol. 1 (Berlin: Dietz Verlag, 1968), 92. One can find similar problems in contemporary Marxism; for instance, Ernest Mandel argued for a "democratic-centralist planning under a national congress of workers' councils made up in its large majority of real workers" (Ernest Mandel, "Economics of the Transition Period," in *50 Years of World Revolution*, edited by Ernest Mandel (New York: Pathfinder Press, 1971), 286. In later writings, he refers rather to "producers/consumers." I often quote from the writings of Ernest Mandel, because he is the most articulate socialist theoretician of democratic planning, but it should be said that until the late 1980s he did not include the ecological issue as a central aspect of his economic arguments.

10.   Ernest Mandel defined planning in the following terms: "An economy governed by a plan implies . . . that society's relatively scarce resources are not apportioned blindly ('behind the backs of the producer-consumer') by the play of the law of value but that they are consciously allocated according to previously established priorities. In a transitional economy where socialist democracy prevails, the mass of the working people democratically determine this choice of priorities" ("Economics of the Transition Period," 282).

11.   "From the point of view of the mass of workers, sacrifices imposed by bureaucratic arbitrariness are neither more nor less 'acceptable' than sacrifices imposed by the blind mechanisms of the market. These represent only two different forms of the same alienation" (ibid., 285).

12.   In his remarkable recent book on socialism, the Argentinian Marxist economist Claudio Katz emphasized that democratic planning, supervised from below by the majority of the population, "is not identical with absolute centralisation, total statisation, war communism or command economy. The transition requires the primacy of planning over the market, but not the suppression of the market variables. The com-

bination between both instances should be adapted to each situation and each country.' However, 'the aim of the socialist process is not to keep an unchanged equilibrium between the plan and the market, but to promote a progressive loss of the market positions" (*El porvenir del socialismo*, Buenos Aires: Herramienta/Imago Mundi, 2004, 47–48).

13. Engels, *Anti-Dühring*, 349.

14. Kovel, *Enemy of Nature*, 215.

15. Ernest Mandel, *Power and Money* (London: Verso, 1991), 209.

16. Mandel observed: "We do not believe that the 'majority is always right.' . . . Everybody does make mistakes. This will certainly be true of the majority of citizens, of the majority of the producers, and of the majority of the consumers alike. But there will be one basic difference between them and their predecessors. In any system of unequal power . . . those who make the wrong decisions about the allocation of resources are rarely those who pay for the consequences of their mistakes. . . . Provided there exists real political democracy, real cultural choice and information, it is hard to believe that the majority would prefer to see their woods die . . . or their hospitals understaffed, rather than rapidly to correct their mistaken allocations" (Ernest Mandel, "In Defense of Socialist Planning," *New Left Review* 1/159, 1986, 31).

17. Mandel, *Power and Money*, 204.

18. Michael Albert, *Participatory Economics: Life After Capitalism* (London: Verso, 2003), 154.

19. For a selection of "negative growth" texts, see Majid Rahnema and Victoria Bawtree, eds., *The Post-Development Reader* (Atlantic Highlands, NJ: Zed Books, 1997), and Michel Bernard et al., eds., *Objectif Décroissance: vers une société harmonieuse* (Lyon: Éditions Parangon, 2004). The main French theorist of décroissance is Serge Latour, author of *La planète des naufragés, essai sur l'après-dévéloppement* (Paris: La Decouverte, 1991).

20. Ernest Mandel was skeptical of rapid changes in consumer habits, such as the private car: "If, in spite of every environmental and other argument, they [the producers and consumers] wanted to maintain the dominance of the private motor car and to continue polluting their

cities, that would be their right. Changes in long-standing consumer orientations are generally slow—there can be few who believe that workers in the United States would abandon their attachment to the automobile the day after a socialist revolution" ("In Defense of Socialist Planning," 30). While Mandel is right in insisting that changes in consumption patterns are not to be imposed, he seriously underestimates the impact that a system of extensive and free-of-charge public transports would have, as well as the assent of the majority of the citizens—already existing today in several great European cities—for measures restricting automobile circulation.

21. Mandel, *Power and Money*, 206.

22. Daniel Singer, *Whose Millennium? Theirs or Ours?* (New York: Monthly Review Press, 1999), 259–60.

23. See S. Baierle, "The Porto Alegre Thermidor," in *Socialist Register 2003*, edited by Leo Panitch and Colin Leys (Pontypool, Wales: Merlin Press, 2003).

24. Walter Benjamin, *Gesammelte Schriften*, vol. 1/3 (Frankfurt: Suhrkamp, 1980), 1232.

25. Patrick Le Lay, quoted in *L'Espress*, July 9, 2004.

26. Chico Mendes, quoted by Ailton Krenak, coordinator of the União das Nações Indígenas (Union of Indigenous Nations) of Brazil. In *Chico Mendes* (São Paulo: Sindicato dos Trabalhadores de Xapuri, Central Unica dos Trabalhadores, 1989).

27. Ibid.

28. Chico Mendes, *Chico Mendes por êle mesmo* (Rio de Janeiro: FASE, 1989), 24.

29. Krenak, *Chico Mendes*, 21.

30. Mendes, *Chico Mendes*, 57.

31. Traven, B., *The White Rose* (Westport, CT: Lawrence Hill, 1979).

32. Information in this section is extracted from a 2012 issue of the Peruvian journal *Lucha Indígena*, edited by the Peruvian indigenous leader and ecosocialist Hugo Blanco.

33. Achim Brunnengräber, "Crise de l'environnement ou crise de société? De l'économie politique du changement climatique" (Environmental

Crisis or Social Crisis? The Political Economy of Climate Change), in *Globalisation et crise écologique. Une critique de l'économie politique par des écologistes allemands* (*Globalization and Ecological Crisis: A Critique of Political Economy by German Ecologists*), edited by Ulrich Brand and Michael Löwy (Paris: L'Harmattan, 2011), 243–62.

34. Matthieu Le Quang, *Laissons le pétrole sous terre. L'initiative Yasuní ITT en Équateur* (Leave the Petroleum in the Ground: the Yasuní ITT Initiative in Ecuador) (Paris: Éditions Omniscience, 2012).

35. World People's Conference on Climate Change and the Rights of Mother Earth, "People's Agreement of Cochabamba," adopted April 22, 2010, http://pwccc.wordpress.com/2010/04/24/peoples-agreement.

36. Denis Chartier and Nathalie Blanc, "Les développements durables de l'Amazonie" (Sustainable Development in the Amazon), in *Grands barrages et habitants. Les risques sociaux du développement* (*Large Dams and Populations: The Social Risks of Development*), edited by N. Blanc and S. Bonin (Paris: Éditions QAUE, 2008), 169–89; A. Hall and S. Brandford, "Development, Dams and Dilma: The Saga of Belo Monte," *Critical Sociology* 38 (2012): 851–62.

Index

"Passim" (literally "scattered") indicates intermittent discussion of a topic over a cluster of pages.

Acosta, Alberto, 68
accumulation of capital, 2, 7, 20, 22, 42, 44, 49, 78
accumulation of goods, 2, 7, 9, 12, 32, 35, 44, 51, 86
"actually existing socialism." See socialism, "nonecological"/"actually existing"/"first-epoch"
Adbusters, 49
advertising, 10, 31, 33–34, 43–51
Africa, 14
agribusiness, 33, 53–54, 55, 62, 63, 72, 75, 91
agriculture, 33, 34, 85, 91. See also agribusiness
AIDESEP. See Interethnic Association for the Development of the Peruvian Rainforest (AIDESEP)
Albert, Michael, 29–31
Alliance pour la Planète (France), 46
The Alternative (Bahro), xii
Altvater, Elmar, 6, 20
Alves da Silva, Darly, 58, 59
Amazonia, 53–59, 63–69 passim, 72, 103
Anarchist Social Ecology (Bookchin), xi
Angus, Ian, xiii, 83, 93
Anti-Dühring (Engels), 21
Arana, Marcos, 64, 66
Ariès, Paul, xi
arms industry, 10, 32
artificial needs. See false needs
Asociación Interétnica de Desarrollo de la Selva Peruana. See Interethnic Association for the Development of the Peruvian Rainforest (AIDESEP)

111

assassination, 16, 55, 59, 66
austerity measures, 32, 48, 50
Australia, ix
automobile industry, 4, 11, 26, 30
automobiles, 10–12 passim, 28, 30, 34, 35, 38, 50, 107–8n20

Bagarollo, Tiziano, 4
Bahro, Rudolf, xii, 6
Bali Climate Change Conference, 2007, 88
banks, ix, 9, 24, 43, 57, 72, 90. See also World Bank
Belém Declaration, xii–xiii, 83–98
Belém World Social Forum, 2009. See World Social Forum: Belém, 2009
Belgium, 5
Belo Monte Dam, 72
Benjamin, Walter, 3, 21, 39
biodiversity, 1, 53, 67, 68, 70
Blanco, Hugo, xiv, 15–16, 64, 66
Bloch, Ernst, xiii, 4
Bolivia, xiv, 54, 64, 65, 69–74 passim, 84
Bolshevik Revolution. See Russian Revolution
Bookchin, Murray: Anarchist Social Ecology, xi
Bové, José, 17
Brasiléia Rural Workers' Union, 54
Brazil, xiii, xiv, 15–17 passim, 38, 53–59, 63–65, 72, 103
Buey, Francisco Fernández, xii, 6
Bureau de Verification de la

Publicité (France), 46
Bush, George W., vii

Canada, ix, xiii, 11
"cap and trade" system. See emissions trading
Capital (Marx), 21, 24
capital accumulation. See accumulation of capital
capitalism, vii, x, 1–9 passim, 21, 42; advertising and, 43–51; Belém Declaration on, 84–91 passim; clash with Indigenous culture, 62; Cochabamba conference statement on, 70; "Ecosocialist Manifesto" on, 77–80; Lima Ecosocialist Declaration on, 102; viewed from future, 100. See also "green capitalism"
Capitalism Nature Socialism, xii, 6
carbon dioxide, ix, 41, 50, 53, 67–68, 86–88 passim
cars. See automobiles
catastrophe, vii, 1, 2, 5, 42, 51, 77, 79; Belém Declaration on, 85, 87; Lima Ecosocialist Declaration on, 101–3 passim; viewed from future, 99. See also Chernobyl nuclear accident, 1986
Catholic Church, 56, 64
cattle ranching. See ranchers and ranching
Chavez, Hugo, 73

Chernobyl nuclear accident, 1986, x, 22

Chile, 72

China, ix, xiv

"clean capitalism." *See* "green capitalism"

climate change. *See* global warming

climate change conferences. *See* United Nations: Framework Convention on Climate Change, COP20, Lima, 2014; United Nations: International Conference on Climate Change, Copenhagen, 2009; World People's Conference on Climate Change, Cochabamba, 2010

coal, 23, 102

Cochabamba Climate Change Conference, 2010. *See* World People's Conference on Climate Change, Cochabamba, 2010

collective ownership, 7, 20, 21, 33, 89, 90

commodification, 17, 44, 46, 64

commodity fetishism, 8, 28, 35, 42, 43, 44, 51

Commoner, Barry, xii, 6

common good, 9, 24, 43, 90

Communist Party of Brazil, 55

competition, ix, 8, 12, 23, 35, 37, 42, 70, 91, 100

Conga Project, 66, 103

conspicuous consumption, viii, 7, 32, 34, 49

consumerism, x, 35, 43, 48, 50, 78

consumers' councils and federations, 29–30, 48

consumer society, 44–45

consumption, viii–xi passim, 7–10 passim, 24, 28–35 passim, 43–51 passim, 78, 91, 107–8n20

Copenhagen Climate Change Conference. *See* United Nations: International Conference on Climate Change, Copenhagen, 2009

"Copenhagen 2049," 99–100

Correa, Rafael, 68, 74, 103

dams, 72

debt, international, 12, 33, 68, 78

"Declaration of Indigenous Peoples" (2009), 63–64

deforestation, 16, 55, 57, 63, 75, 84

Deléage, Jean-Paul, xii, 6

democratic management. *See* workers' self-management

democratic planning, 9, 19–39 passim, 90, 106–7nn9–12 passim

Democratic Rural Union (UDR) (Brazil), 55

demonstrations, Latin American. *See* protests, Latin American

desertification, 1, 42, 99, 101

desires, 35, 44, 50, 81

direct democracy, 28, 36, 89, 107n6

disease, 84, 85

distribution policy, 9, 24

drought, 1, 42, 85

ecological catastrophe. *See* catastrophe

ecological crisis, 7, 37, 41, 79, 85–87 passim, 101–3 passim

"ecology of the poor," 14–16

eco-Marxism, xi, 4

economic growth, vii, viii, 2, 7, 42, 79, 84–86 passim, 100; advertising role in, 51; compared to Indigenous model, 71. *See also* "negative growth"

economic planning, democratic. *See* democratic planning

economic planning, nondemocratic. *See* planned economy, nondemocratic

Ecosocialist Conference, Belém, 2009, 64

Ecosocialist International Network, 92, 99, 101–3

"Ecosocialist Manifesto" (Kovel and Löwy), xii, 77–82

eco-taxes, 5, 11

Ecuador, 64–74 passim, 103

elections, 28, 38, 66, 68

El Salvador, 72

emission-avoidance agreements, 67–68

emissions trading, ix, 68, 87, 88, 100

energy, nuclear. *See* nuclear energy

energy, renewable. *See* renewable energy

energy consumption, 7

energy policy, 9, 23, 43, 71, 90, 91

Engels, Friedrich, 2, 3, 26; *Anti-Dühring*, 21

environmental catastrophe. *See* catastrophe

environmental crisis. *See* ecological crisis

equality. *See* gender equality; inequality

Europe, ix, xi–xii, 4, 5, 38, 68, 108n20; nuclear disasters, x, 22; viewed from future, 99–100. *See also* France

Europe's Green Alternative, xii

exchange value, 7, 20, 26, 81, 89

false needs, 33, 34, 43–44

farmers' movement, 17

fashion, 32, 49

fishing industry, 23, 37, 73

Follett, Danielle, 83, 99

food, 32, 33, 43, 89, 91, 92; contamination, 1, 12, 17. *See also* agriculture

Forest Peoples Alliance, 15, 16, 56–59 passim

forests, tropical. *See* rainforests

fossil fuels, 23, 28, 68, 73, 81, 102. *See also* oil industry; oil reserves

Foster, John Bellamy, xiii, xiv, 6, 20, 105n5

Fourier, Charles, 3

Fourth International, xii

Framework Convention on Climate Change, COP20, Lima, 2014. *See* United Nations: Framework Convention on Climate

Change, COP20, Lima, 2014
France, xii, xiii, 5, 17, 46, 47
free or inexpensive transportation, 12, 28, 34–35, 91, 108n20
free or subsidized goods, 9, 24
free-trade agreements, 65
Fukushima nuclear accident, 2011, x

García, Alan, 65
García Linera, Álvaro, 74
gas. *See* natural gas
gender equality, 90
genetic engineering and GMOs, 1, 11, 14, 17, 33, 37, 46, 75; Belém Declaration on, 92
The German Ideology (Marx), ix
Germany, xii, 4, 5, 68
global South. *See* Southern Hemisphere
global warming, vii–viii, 1, 11, 23, 27, 41–42, 49, 68, 82–89 passim; automobiles and, 34, 50; conferences, ix, xiii, xiv, 69–71, 75, 88, 100–103; Latin America and, 53, 73–75 passim; Lima Ecosocialist Declaration on, 101–3 passim; viewed from future, 99. *See also* greenhouse gas emission
GMOs. *See* genetic engineering and GMOs
gold mines, 66
good, common. *See* common good
goods, accumulation. *See* accumulation of goods
goods, free or subsidized goods. *See* free or subsidized goods
goods, shoddiness of. *See* shoddiness of goods
Gorz, André, xii, xiii, 5, 6, 20
"green capitalism," xiii, 5, 8, 11, 37, 42, 91
greenhouse gas emission, ix, 11, 37, 41, 47, 67–68, 91, 100; offsets, 87–88
green parties, xi, xii, 5, 10, 20
greenwashing, 46, 78

Hansen, James: *Storms of My Grandchildren*, vii–viii
Harper, James, 99
health, 12, 14, 62, 85
Hegel, G. W. F., 10
highway construction, resistance to. *See* resistance to highway construction
Humala, Ollanta, 66
humanism, 6, 8, 10
human desires. *See* desires
human needs. *See* needs
hydrochlorofluorocarbons (HCFCs), 11, 37

ice sheets and ice caps, melting of, 1, 41, 85, 99, 101
IMF. *See* International Monetary Fund
imperialism, 3, 33, 70–86 passim; advertising as, 48
Indigenous peoples, xiv, 61–76

passim, 90, 92, 103; Brazil, 16, 53, 56, 57, 59

"Indigenous Peoples' Declaration." *See* "Declaration of Indigenous Peoples" (2009)

industrial fishing. *See* fishing industry

inequality, 7, 8, 78, 85

Inter-American Development Bank, 57

Interethnic Association for the Development of the Peruvian Rainforest (AIDESEP), 65–66

International Conference on Climate Change, Copenhagen, 2009. *See* United Nations: International Conference on Climate Change, Copenhagen, 2009

international debt. *See* debt, international

International Ecosocialist Network (IEN), xii, xiii, xiv

International Monetary Fund, 12

Italy, 5, 68

Japan, x, 11

Juquin, Pierre, xii

Katz, Claudio, 106–7n12

Kempf, Hervé, viii

Kovel, Joel, xiii, xiv, 20, 26, 93, 99; "Ecosocialist Manifesto," xii, 77–82

Kyoto accords, ix, 11, 68, 87–88

labor movement, 5, 6, 12, 16. *See also* unions

Landless Workers' Movement (MST), 17, 38, 56

Latin America, xiv, 15, 61–76, 103. *See also* Bolivia; Brazil

leisure, 2, 12, 25, 35

liberation theology. *See* theology of liberation

Lima Ecosocialist Declaration, 101–3

Lipietz, Alain, 5–6

logging, 23, 47, 65

Lula da Silva, Luiz Inácio, 55, 72

Luxemburg, Rosa, 79, 80

Mandel, Ernest, 28, 29, 35–36, 106nn9–11, 107n16

marketing, 43

Márkus, György, 25

Martínez-Alier, Joan, 6, 14

Marx, Karl, 2, 3, 4, 19, 22, 105n5; *Capital*, 21, 24; *The German Ideology*, ix; view of leisure, 2, 25, 35, 44

Marxists and Marxism, xi, xii, 2–10 passim, 20, 21, 37, 54, 106n9

Maxus Energy Corporation, 67

media, 45, 46

Mendes, Chico, 15–16, 54–59, 72

methane, 85

Mexico, xiv

Mientras Tanto, xii

militarism, 53, 66, 70, 78. *See also*

war
mining, 15, 61–66 passim, 74, 75,
    103
Monsanto, 17
Monthly Review, xiii
"moral economics," 42
Morales, Evo, 69, 73–74, 84
Morris, William, 105n5
"Mother Earth," 69, 70, 71
Movimento dos Trabalhadores
    Rurais Sem Terra. *See* Landless
    Workers' Movement (MST)

Naess, Arne, xi
National Council of Seringueiros
    (Brazil), 56, 58
"natural" catastrophes, 1, 42
natural gas, 73, 74, 102
needs, 26, 32–36 passim, 43–44,
    50, 71, 81
"negative growth," 32
Newmont, 66
Nicaragua, 72
nonviolent resistance, 55
North-South relations, 7, 12–14
    passim, 33, 67–69, 86, 88, 92
Norway, 68
nuclear accidents, x, 1, 22, 23
nuclear energy, ix–x, 22, 23, 30,
    46, 91
nuclear waste, 23

Obama, Barack, ix
Objecteurs de Croissance, 49
Observatory of Latin American

Mining Conflicts (OCMAL),
    65, 66
ocean level, 42, 85, 99–100, 101
O'Connor, James, xii, 3–4, 7, 20
October Revolution. *See* Russian
    Revolution
oil industry, 11, 23, 34, 61–75
    passim, 82, 103
oil reserves, 7
oligarchy, viii, 2, 25, 58–59, 68,
    73, 74
One-Way Street (Benjamin), 3
On the Concept of History
    (Benjamin), 3
ozone layer depletion, 1, 11, 37

participatory democracy. *See* direct
    democracy
"participatory economy" (parecon),
    29–31
Partido dos Trabalhadores (PT).
    See Workers' Party (PT)
    (Brazil)
Pastoral Land Commission
    (Brazil), 56
peasant movements, 15–16, 33, 53–
    66 passim, 75. *See also* Landless
    Workers' Movement (MST)
People's Conference on Climate
    Change, Cochabamba, 2010.
    See World People's Conference
    on Climate Change,
    Cochabamba, 2010
permafrost, 41, 85
Peru, 15, 64–67 passim, 103

petroleum industry. *See* oil industry

petroleum reserves. *See* oil reserves

Pinheiro, Wilson, 54

planned economy, democratic. *See* democratic planning

planned economy, nondemocratic, 45

planned obsolescence of goods, 32, 43, 91

Polanyi, Karl, 9

polar ice cap melting, 1, 41

police: South America, 55, 66

pollution, ix, 1, 9–15 passim, 27, 34, 37, 66, 78; Belém Declaration on, 84, 90, 91; credits-trading, 87–88; "export," 13–14; Lima Ecosocialist Declaration on, 102; Peru, 15. *See also* water pollution

Porto Alegre, Brazil, 38. *See also* World Social Forum: Porto Alegre, 2001

Prestes, Luís Carlos, 54

prices, 24, 30

production, xi, 2–4 passim, 9, 10, 23–24, 42, 45, 51; Belém Declaration on, 84, 85, 89, 90, 91; collective ownership, 89; means, 20, 24, 26, 43, 80, 89, 90; in parecon, 30, 31; profit-oriented, 85; Soviet Union, 21–22; viewed from future, 100

productivism, xi, 2–10 passim, 20–22 passim, 32, 80–81, 88, 89

profit, 8, 19, 26, 42–45 passim, 62, 78, 84, 85; Lima Ecosocialist Declaration on, 101, 102

protests, Latin American, 15, 53, 65, 66, 68, 73, 74, 100

public health. *See* health

public transportation, 11, 12, 28, 34–35, 37, 91, 108

radioactive waste. *See* nuclear waste

rail transport, 35, 37, 91

rainforests, 1, 15, 23, 53–67 passim, 72–75 passim, 103

ranchers and ranching, 54, 55, 63, 72

rationality, 10

reforms and reformism, 5, 8, 11, 12, 19–21 passim, 37, 43, 81; agrarian, 57, 59; Belém Declaration on, 85, 87, 91; Lima Ecosocialist Declaration on, 103

religion, 61, 62. *See also* theology of liberation

renewable energy, x, 9, 23, 32, 33, 43, 68, 89, 90. *See also* solar energy

repression, political/state, 45, 66, 67, 78

repression of desires, 35, 44, 81

resistance to highway construction, 74

revolution, 22, 38, 82, 88, 89; Benjamin view, 39; Foster view, 105n5; Mendes dream, 56–57

Riechmann, Jorge, 6, 13, 104
Rousseff, Dilma, 72
Russian Revolution, 22
rubber-tappers, 16, 54–59 passim

Sacristán, Manuel, xi, xii
Saul, Quincy, xiii
Seattle WTO protests, 2009, xiv, 16, 37, 92
self-management. *See* workers' self-management
shoddiness of goods, 45. *See also* planned obsolescence
Silva, Marina, 72
Singer, Daniel: *Whose Millennium?*, 36
Smith, Richard, 19
socialism, "nonecological"/"actually existing"/"first-epoch," xi, 5, 6, 80–81
socialist planning. *See* democratic planning
solar energy, 23, 28, 31
Southern Hemisphere, 10, 13, 33, 85, 87, 92, 102. *See also* North–South relations
Soviet Union, 20–22, 25
Spain, xi, xii, 4, 68
"sponsorship" (advertising), 46
Storms of My Grandchildren (Hansen), vii–viii
subsidies, 9, 24, 28
Summers, Lawrence, 13–14
supply and demand, 24, 30, 43

Tavora, Euclides Fernandes, 54
taxation, 5, 11, 28, 37, 51
technology, 15, 19–26 passim, 31, 58; Bagarollo view, 4; Benjamin view, 3; Obama/EU view, ix; optimistic view, 32; reorientation/social regulation, 7, 9, 20, 26, 43, 90. *See also* nuclear energy
television: France, 46
Texaco, 67
theology of liberation, 54, 64
Thompson, E. P., 8, 42
Tobin tax, 51
totalitarianism, 22, 25
toxic waste, 14, 27. *See also* nuclear waste
trade unions. *See* unions
transportation policy, 9, 12, 28, 30, 34–38 passim, 50–51, 91, 108n20. *See also* automobiles
Traven, B.: *The White Rose*, 62–63
trucking industry, 35, 37, 91

União Democrática Ruralista. *See* Democratic Rural Union (UDR) (Brazil)
unions, xiv, 12, 48, 61, 75; Brazil, 16, 54–58 passim, 73; Europe, 4
United Nations, xiii, 16, 57; Framework Convention on Climate Change, COP20, Lima, 2014, 101–3; International Conference on Climate

Change, Copenhagen, 2009,
xiii, 69, 100
United Nations Development Programme (UNDP), 67–68
United States, ix, 13, 78; cars, 35,
108n20; ecosocialist pioneers,
xi–xii; energy consumption, 7;
free-trade agreements, 65
Uruguay, 72
use value, 2, 7, 20, 26, 81, 89
USSR. *See* Soviet Union
utopia, 10, 11, 36–37

Veblen, Thorstein, viii, 49
Venezuela, 73, 74

wants. *See* desires
war, 77, 91
waste (industrial, etc.), 1, 84. *See
also* toxic waste
wastefulness of production and
consumption, 7, 9, 32, 34,
47, 78, 84, 91
water pollution, 15, 66, 75
weather, extreme, 1, 85, 101
Weber, Max, 62
The White Rose (Traven), 62–63
Whose Millennium? (Singer), 36
Williams, Raymond, xi–xii, 6
Wolf, Frieder Otto, xii, 6
women's movements, 90
workers' councils and federations,
29–30, 106n9
Workers' Party (PT) (Brazil), 55–56
workers' self-management, 26, 27,

29, 30, 102, 103
work time, 12, 28
World Bank, 12, 88
World People's Conference on Cli-
mate Change, Cochabamba,
2010, xiv, 69–71, 75
World Social Forum, 37; Belém,
2009, xiii, 63–65, 83; Porto
Alegre, 2001, 16–17, 63
World Trade Organization
protests, Seattle, 2009. *See*
Seattle WTO protests, 2009

Xapuri Rural Workers' Union, 55

Yanacocha, 66
Yasuní National Park, Ecuador,
67–69, 74, 103

About the Author

Michael Löwy, born in Brazil in 1938, has lived in Paris since 1969. Presently he is research director emeritus at the National Center for Scientific Research. His books and articles have been translated into twenty-eight languages. He is a coauthor, with Joel Kovel, of the International Ecosocialist Manifesto (2001). Among his main publications: *Fire Alarm: Reading Walter Benjamin's "On the Concept of History"* (London: Verso, 2005), *The Theory of Revolution in the Young Marx* (Chicago: Haymarket Books, 2009), *On Changing the World: Essays in Political Philosophy, from Karl Marx to Walter Benjamin* (Chicago: Haymarket Books, 2012); and *Ecosocialisme : Une alternative radicale à la catastrophe écologique capitaliste* (Paris: Fayard, 2012).